THE ULTIMATE GUIDE TO
Surfcasting

Ron Arra releases the cast that set a new U.S. record and regained him his national title at the Stren Longcasting Championships at Marco Island, Florida in 1988. Arra has a personal best of 758.44 feet in Sportcast USA competition.

S THE ULTIMATE GUIDE TO *urfcasting*

Ron Arra and Curt Garfield
Foreword by Nelson Bryant

The Lyons Press
Guilford, Connecticut
An imprint of The Globe Pequot Press

The Lyons Press is an imprint of The Globe Pequot Press.

Printed in Canada

Designed by Compset, Inc.

2 4 6 8 10 9 7 5 3

Library of Congress Cataloging-in-Publication Data

Arra, Ron.
    The ultimate guide to surfcasting / Ron Arra and Curt Garfield ;
foreword by Nelson Bryant.
        p. cm.
    ISBN 1-58574-299-6
    1. Surfcasting. I. Garfield, Curt. II. Title

SH454.7 .A78 2001
799.1'6—dc21

                                                            2001038919

Contents

Foreword   vii

Introduction   1

  1. *The Right Gear*   3

  2. *The Pendulum Principle*   15

  3. *Casting Techniques*   19

  4. *Taking Care of Your Gear and Yourself*   47

  5. *Ten Tips for More Distance*   51

  6. *Rigging for That Faraway Fish*   61

  7. *Long-Distance Fishing*   71

  8. *Start Youngsters Off Right*   77

  9. *The Two-Handed Fly Rod Finds a Home*   83

 10. *Stan Gibbs: Still the Master*   97

 11. *The Proof of the Pudding*   101

 12. *The Tournament Trail*   105

 13. *Tune Up for More Distance*   117

Appendices

A. Sources for Equipment   127

B. Eelskin Rigs   129

C. For the Record   133

Foreword

Those who are truly serious in their desire to increase the distance they can heave a lure out over the pounding surf will welcome this new handbook by Ron Arra and Curt Garfield.

A decade ago, Arra and Garfield teamed up to produce *Power Surfcasting*, a primer on how the average angler, using the pendulum-type cast or variations of it, can learn to cast consistently, if he or she is diligent, well over one hundred yards.

This new book explains and illustrates the method in greater detail and also ventures into other areas, including long, two-handed fly rods for saltwater fishing from shore, whether in the surf or in rocky, brushy areas where there isn't much room for a backcast.

The key to the pendulum technique is a smooth buildup of power that fully loads the rod. It's a matter of timing that is similar to the backcast in fly fishing. The book also describes a modified version of the pendulum cast that doesn't achieve as much distance, but is easier to learn. The full and modified pendulum casts can be done with spinning gear, but greater yardage is gained with a proper revolving-spool reel and a rod of eleven feet or more with a firm butt section.

Some might ask why they should spend much time learning how to reach out an additional twenty, thirty, or forty yards, because in many instances the fish—whether blues or stripers—are right against the beach. The urge to make a long cast is a blend of the psychological and the practical. There's no denying the pleasure in strolling down to the water's edge with other anglers on either side of you and uncorking a cast that goes far beyond anything they are achieving, and, of course, there are times when the fish are breaking far offshore and no one else can reach them.

The ability to make really long casts can occasionally mean the difference between succeeding or failing in your quest. It's somewhat akin to my putting a half dozen magnum BB goose loads in my pocket when I go duck hunting in a little cove at the head of a salt pond in winter. When decoying ducks—mallards or black ducks are my usual visitors—I use standard loads and No. 6 shot for them, but once or twice a season a half dozen Canada geese will fly past forty or fifty yards away, and the lighter loads and smaller shot wouldn't suffice.

Hooking a big bluefish or striper 100 or 150 yards away has its problems, however, particularly if you are standing virtually shoulder to shoulder with other anglers and a strong tide is running. Once you are fast to your fish you will be unable to bring it directly to you—as you might be able to do with a shorter line—and you will have to march downtide along the shore, forcing every angler on that side of you to reel in and get out of your way.

It takes a lot of effort and time to get a fish that has been hooked at the end of a long cast to the beach. Perhaps it's because I'm getting long in the tooth, but when surfcasting I generally throw my lure no farther than the closest fish, unless I think that there might be some larger specimens lurking about offshore.

Arra and Garfield devote an excellent chapter to long-distance fighting of fish from shore when other anglers are about, and there's good advice about what to do in the closing moments of the game when the quarry must be eased ashore.

It is my feeling that the average surf fisherman will use the information in this book to improve his casting ability, perhaps picking up another twenty or thirty yards, but for those inspired to excel, or perhaps even to take part in tournament casting, all the needed information is here, including choosing rods, reels, and lines, whether for conventional or spinning outfits.

There are detailed instructions on how to spool line on a conventional reel for tournament casting, how to test that reel for balance, and how to fine-tune it, whether it has magnets, brake blocks, or both.

Arra is a passionate teacher who loves to fish as much as he loves to cast, and he has even rigged a bicycle to carry rods and gear as he prowls the banks of his beloved Cape Cod Canal in quest of striped bass. His fascination with fishing began early on during trips with his father such as the one related in this book: As a twelve-year-old, bottom fishing for stripers with cut mackerel and sand worms as bait off Sandy Neck Beach on Cape Cod before dawn. A little before sunup, a fish took the bait on one of the rods they had set in sand spikes, and, with a little help from his dad, Ron beached a thirty-nine-inch striper, his first, and was hooked as deeply as the fish.

Tips for those as interested in catching fish as they are in the long toss are abundant, including how to fish jigs and the venerable eel-skin rig. There's even a chapter on Cape Cod's Stan Gibbs, now 86, a master luremaker who began fashioning plugs in his Sagamore home in 1945, lures that soon were catching more fish and fishermen than any others of their genre.

When I first watched Arra cast—throwing about seven hundred feet across a Martha's Vineyard meadow back in the late 1980s—I witnessed an exciting, as befits a one-time professional athlete who trains hard at his craft, blend of power and grace and knew that I had neither the dedication nor, probably, the coordination to achieve such mastery. I did, however, use some of his techniques to increase my average toss with a surf rod by a hundred feet or more, no stunning achievement, but just about what I wanted.

Nelson Bryant
Martha's Vineyard
July 2001

Ron Arra's heavy-duty Canal fishing bike. Bike is a women's model, easier to climb on and off, and features PVC pipe rod holders and three baskets for gear and to carry home a big striper. Two kickstands prevent the bike from falling over in windy conditions, helping to protect rods and equipment.

Introduction

IN THE UNITED STATES, THE NAME RON ARRA IS SYNONYMOUS with long-distance casting. Ron Arra has won five national Long-Distance Casting titles and dominated Distance Casting competition in this country for nearly a decade before finally retiring from competition in 1989.

This book is not intended to make the reader a Distance Casting champion, although there is a chapter on techniques and equipment for tournament casting. This book's intent is to teach the surf angler a technique that will increase distance by at least one hundred feet and cover more water with far less effort.

The successful surf angler may well say "Why bother? I'm catching plenty of fish right now." But few are the surf fishermen who haven't had occasion to look on helplessly as a school of gamefish scatter bait just beyond the reach of their best cast. Arra has helped anglers of all ages from as far away as Florida and the United Kingdom develop techniques that allow them to cast further with less than half the effort of their original casting style.

Frustration at not being able to reach fish holding in the middle of the Cape Cod Canal or beyond the Sandwich Bar led Ron to modify the pendulum casting techniques brought to this country from England by John Holden, into a style all his own. Following the first round of the 1989 Stren Regionals, Ron became the first man ever to cast all the way across the Canal, a distance, at that point, (the Coal Yard) of nearly eight hundred feet.

Ron has cast 850 feet unofficially on the practice field. His longest official effort was 758.44 feet in 1987 at a Sportcast USA sanctioned tournament in Falmouth, Massachusetts.

Reading this book probably won't make the reader proficient enough to duplicate that feat, although it's not out of the realm of possibility with the right equipment, 100 percent dedication and a lot of practice. What this book *will* do is help the angler interested in getting more distance select the right equipment and learn casting techniques that will get the most out of it with the least amount of physical effort.

Size, youth, and brute strength take a back seat in importance to technique, balance, graceful smoothness, and timing. Anyone of any size and physical condition can learn how to cast for distance. It's just a question of letting the rod do the work for you. Turn the pages and we'll show you how.

1

The Right Gear

LET'S GET SOMETHING STRAIGHT RIGHT UP FRONT. I'VE NEVER hooked a fish on my 13½-foot Zziplex distance competition rod and it certainly wouldn't be any fun even if I did. The rod is just too rigid and stiff from two feet below the tip to the butt end. The true tournament rod is designed for casting only and doesn't have the continuous flex needed to retrieve a fish properly. We'll talk about tournament casting equipment and techniques in a later chapter. For now, let's concentrate on long-distance fishing.

Lamiglas and many other manufacturers are producing blanks and finished rods designed for use with the modified pendulum technique. They'll help you get your lure or bait to where the fish are holding and they have a moderate flex action that will allow you to play a fish effectively once it's hooked.

For all-around surf fishing using conventional gear, I like a one- or two-piece graphite rod between 10 and 11½ feet long with a fast to moderate action—that is one that has a gradual bend from mid-section to the tip-top—and a flexible but firm butt section which curves along one-third to one-half of the blank. Be wary of a rod that

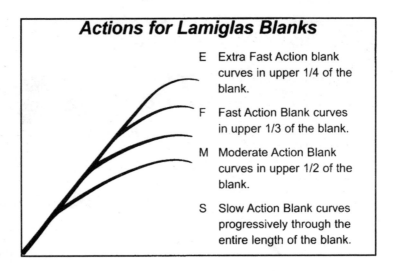

Actions for Lamiglas Blanks

E   Extra Fast Action blank curves in upper 1/4 of the blank.

F   Fast Action Blank curves in upper 1/3 of the blank.

M   Moderate Action Blank curves in upper 1/2 of the blank.

S   Slow Action Blank curves progressively through the entire length of the blank.

bends too much toward the tip. A fast action is ideal for the off-the-beach cast and it can be used for modified pendulum casting also.

For ultimate distance with conventional gear I want an extra-fast-action blank that curves in its upper quarter. For plug casting I prefer the Lamiglas fast-action blank that curves in the upper third of the blank. For jigging I go to the moderate firm action that curves in the upper half. For bait fishing and sand eel rigs, a slow action that curves progressively over the whole length of the blank would be my choice.

Lamiglas is getting a lot of ink in this chapter, and with good reason. The company has been producing top quality fishing rods and blanks for nearly fifty years. Their shop in Woodland, Washington is hard by the North Fork of the Lewis River, home of some of the meanest fish in the West. The company's founders started out by custom-designing rods for local anglers. As the word spread, they started hearing from anglers all over the world.

Lamiglas has pioneered the use of the newest and most technologically advanced materials available, but still makes most of its rods by hand. They fish the rods they build. I test new additions to the Ron Arra Surf Pro Series personally on waters where they have been designed to be fished.

(*Patrick Wiseman photo*)

My surf fishing rods. Bottom to top:

1. *Custom-wrapped Lamiglas conventional XRA 1204 10-foot live eeling and plugging one-piece rod rated for* $^7/_8$*–2$^1/_2$-ounce lures.*

2. *Custom-wrapped XRA 1321 11-foot one-piece spinning rod rated for 1- to 3-ounce lures.*

3. *Custom-wrapped XRA conventional 126 1MH 10-foot, 6-inch one-piece jigging rod rated for 4-6 ounce lures.*

4. *Custom-wrapped conventional XRA 1322 11-foot one-piece rated for 1-5 ounce lures. The ultimate plugging rod.*

5. *Custom-wrapped XRA 1083 9-foot one-piece spinning rod rated for* $^3/_8$*– to 2$^1/_4$-ounce lures. Excellent light tackle and live eeling rod.*

6. *Custom-wrapped conventional XRA 1205 10-foot one-piece rated for 1- to 5$^1/_2$-ounce lures. Excellent all-around surfcasting rod.*

7. *Finished Ron Arra Spinning Surf Pro Model XSRA 1321–2, 11-foot two-piece rated for 1- to 3-ounce lures. Excellent plugging rod.*

8. *Finished Ron Arra Spinning Surf Pro Model XSRA 1322–2, 11-foot two-piece for 1- to 5-ounce lures. Ultimate two-piece plugging rod.*

You'll see competition casters and some surf anglers attaching their reels to their rods with coaster clamps or electrician's tape, but for fishing situations, I prefer a rod fitted with a standard Fuji FS-7SB or FPSD Deluxe low-profile reel seat. This allows me to change reels quickly to adjust to fluctuating fishing conditions. Tough, long-lasting guides that don't nick or groove easily and a Fuji PST silicon carbide tip-top are extremely important. I like the Fuji BNLG, NSG, and the new Fuji Concept Alconite guides for use with conventional surf rods. For spinning rods, the GBSVLG and the Alconite guides are an excellent choice.

There are several excellent reels on the market that work well with the modified pendulum technique. My personal favorite for general beach fishing conditions, where line capacity is not crucial and distance is, is the 6500C3CT from Abu Garcia, a great distance reel with an innovative design in which the spool rotates around a shaft on ball bearings.

If I'm tossing big plugs in the two- to five-ounce range, I'll move up to the Garcia 7000C which is a great night-fishing reel because of its level-wind feature and superb drag system. The Newell P220 is one of my favorite plugging and jigging reels, and the 7500C3CT from Abu Garcia is an excellent choice for casting heavier bait rigs and large plugs. It will take a ton of abuse, as will the Penn 525 MAG and the old standby Penn 140.

While I'll use spinning gear and the 5500C Abu revolving spool reel and the Penn 930 Levelmatic with ultralight lures, casting any lure or bait weighing one ounce or more calls for conventional revolving-spool reels. The Penn 550SS and the new Van Staal VS100, the Daiwa SSII3500C and the Penn 450SS (skirted spool) are excellent saltwater spinning reels for casting very light lures.

The Daiwa 6000T Emblem-X is a good compromise choice for either tournament casting competition or fishing situations. Other good long-distance fishing reels with large line capacity include the Van Staal VS250, the Daiwa 5500A, and the Penn 850SS. On these reels I use 14- to 17-pound-test line with about one-and-a-half times the rod's length of 25- to 30-pound test shock leader.

Heavy-duty conventional surfcasting reels with good line capacity. Clockwise from upper left:

1. Abu 7000 with 50-pound-test FireLine for jigging and eelskinning, line capacity 270 yards, 4.1:1 gear ratio.

2. Abu 7000 C3, line capacity 270 yards of 20-pound-test, 4.1:1 gear ratio.

3. Abu 7500 C3 with 30-pound-test Berkley Big Game line and a 50-pound-test shock leader, 4.1:1 gear ratio. Excellent plugging and baitfishing reel.

4. Abu 7000 with 40-pound-test Big Game line, modified with levelwind mechanism replaced with a solid crossbar, 4.1:1 gear ratio. Used for baitfishing from the beach.

5. Newell Model P220 with 25-pound-test Big Game line and a 40-pound-test shock leader. Line capacity 200 yards of 20-pound-test, 5:1 gear ratio. One of my favorite plugging reels.

6. Penn 525 MAG with 25-pound-test Big Game line and a 40-pound-test shock leader. Line capacity 275 yards of 15-pound-test. An excellent distance plugging reel with a great drag system and a 6:1 gear ratio.

Basic equipment for a beach fishing trip includes lightweight, breathable waders that will keep you cool on hot days and comfortable on long walks. Always bring a hat for wind, rain, and sun protection.

Optional is a lipper tool or BogaGrip to grab and hold a fish for easy, safe landing. A sand spike will hold your surf rod when bottom-fishing with bait. A rope will be of great help for transporting your fish on a long walk.

The surf rod is lightweight graphite with good casting and fishing capabilities. Carry two reels, one for backup, with enough line capacity to handle a running fish.

Two fishing bags are a plus. One carries a variety of swimming plugs and surface poppers, as well as jigs, metal lures, and plastic baits. The other surf bag holds line, hooks, sinkers, and terminal tackle, as well as baits such as bagged and iced sand eels or sea worms.

1. *Penn 850 SS with manual bail. An excellent, reasonably priced surf-casting reel with large line capacity of 325 yards of 20-pound-test mono-filament and a 4.6:1 gear ratio. This rugged reel will take a lot of abuse.*

2. *Daiwa Emblem-X 6000 T. This is the best tournament distance-casting reel and an excellent fishing reel as well. Line capacity 170 yards of 16-pound-test monofilament. Gear ratio 4.6:1.*

3. *Daiwa Emblem 5500 A. A top-notch distance caster for tourna-ments and excellent for fishing as well.*

4. *Van Staal VS 200. A higher-priced reel with a manual bail pickup and roller guide. Excellent for crashing surf and sandy conditions, this reel is sealed and totally waterproof and can be submerged in clean salt water. It also has the ultimate smooth drag system. Line capacity 400 yards of 15-pound-test monofilament. Gear ratio 4.25:1.*

5. *Penn 650 with automatic bail. Excellent for fishing lives eels and swimming lures at night.*

6. *Penn 750 SS with automatic bail. A reasonably priced, top-notch reel that holds 250 yards of 20-pound-test mono. Gear ratio 4.6:1.*

7. *Penn 450 SS with automatic bail. An excellent light-tackle surf-casting reel that holds 250 yards of 10-pound-test monofilament. Gear ratio 5:1.*

On larger conventional reels such as the P220 Newell, 7000 Abu or Penn 140, fill the spool to within an eighth of an inch of the spool flange with a good-quality monofilament or braided line. Most distance casting competitors use Golden Stren, but there are other good brands as well, including Ande and Berkley Trilene Big Game, my personal choice. Top that with at least a 30-pound-test shock leader. I tie on a Dual Lock snap to facilitate changing lures because I think

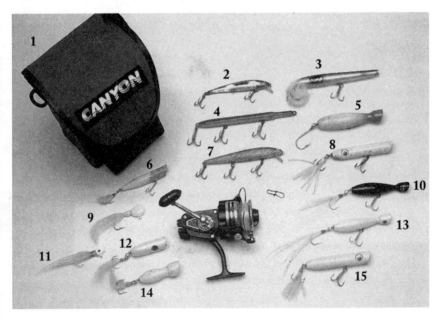

Light–tackle lures:

1. Canyon lure bag.

2. ⅞-ounce Bomber swimming lure, productive at night when retrieved slowly.

3. 1½-ounce Gibbs Pencil Popper, porgy color, very productive when danced across the surface at night. Very attractive to stripers in rocky, shallow-water situations when retrieved slowly.

4. 1¼-ounce blue Gibbs Needlefish, imitates a sand eel. Can be used with a dropper, Redgill, or fly 6 to 10 inches ahead of it. You can also re-

move the rear treble and substitute a feather tied to a single siwash hook. The Needlefish works best at night, retrieved very slowly.

5. 1½-ounce Gibbs Redhead Polaris Popper. One of my favorites for daybreak surface action.

6. 1-ounce blue Atom Popper. Great for estuaries and shallow-water beach fishing any tine of day. Should be retrieved fast.

7. 1-ounce modified color (pink) Rebel swimmer, great night or day retrieved at different speeds. Can also be fished with a dropper.

8. 1½-ounce Habs Squid Popper, great on the surface in early morning or in estuaries on the outgoing tide.

9. 1½-ounce yellow Bill Upperman's jig, very productive in moving water and rough surf. Can be bounced or dragged along a sandy beach bottom.

10, 1¼-ounce Little Trouble black Habs popper, designed to attract fish to the surface from deep structure day or night.

11. 1-ounce leadhead surf jig, used in the same way as the Bill Upperman's jig.

12. 1-ounce Habs popper in pearl color, great all-around popper, especially good for shallow water and drop-offs near sandbars.

13. 1¼-ounce Little Trouble white Habs popper. This is my favorite color for early morning.

14. 1-ounce Little Trouble yellow Habs popper. Excellent when stripers are feeding on porgies and other small baitfish. This lure should be retrieved slowly with an erratic action.

15. 1½-ounce yellow Habs popper. Very productive in all surfcasting situations.

it gives the lure a better action. If I'm using a jig, live eels, or a Redgill with a fish-finder rig, I'll tie a barrel swivel two and one-half feet ahead of the lure to cut down on line twist. When jigging or eelskinning, I use Berkley Power Pro, Whiplash, and Fireline, which is my favorite. All have excellent bite detection while bouncing jigs. I prefer Big Game mono for plug casting.

While the pendulum technique was developed and modified in England primarily for bait fishermen to reach drop-offs five hundred

Popular surfcasting lines, clockwise from top left:

1. Berkley Trilene 30-pound-test Super Strong Big Game monofila-ment, excellent for fishing bait from the beach and casting large plugs without a shock leader.

2. Berkley FireLine 50-pound-test, the same diameter as ordinary 25-pound test monofilament, my favorite for casting jigs and eelskin rigs such as at the Cape Cod Canal where bite detection, strength, and abra-sion resistance are so important.

3. Berkley Whiplash 50-pound-test, the same diameters as ordinary 12-pound test monofilament, great for both spinning and conventional reels because of more line capacity. It has less stretch for improved bite de-tection and offers excellent casting distance and abrasion resistance for fishing in rocky areas.

feet away, most distance surfcasting in the United States is done with plugs—the more aerodynamically shaped the better. Some of my fa-vorites are the Luhr-Jensen Crippled Herring, Habs, Needlefish, Gibbs Skipper and Pencil Popper, Polaris Popper, Super Strike Needlefish, and the Ketch 'n and Fetch from Atom. Obviously, there are others that will cast—and attract fish—equally as well.

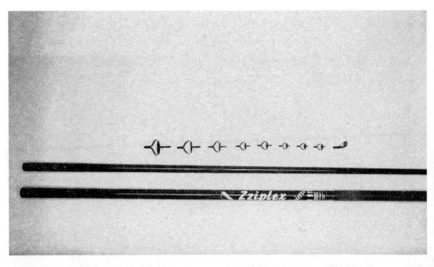

Terry Carroll, owner of Zziplex and a former UK distance surfcasting champion, designed the new Zziplex Primo Phase Taper tournament rod. The blank is a two-piece, dual-taper construction. The rod is 13 feet long and incredibly weighs only 16 ounces. The new Phase Taper design has been proven to offer considerable advantages in the pendulum and off-beach casting techniques.

The guides I recommend for this rod are Fuji Alconite BMNAG ring guides. These guides are so durable they can be made thinner than other ceramic guides, and will hold up under demanding casting and fishing conditions.

Here are recommended guide spacings from the tip down when using a revolving-spool reel: 4 inches; 9 inches; 15 inches; 22 inches; 31 inches; 43 inches; 63 inches; and 93 inches. Ring sizes from the tip down: #10; #10; #12; #12; #16; #20; #25; #30; and a Fuji PST SIC #12 ring.

2

The Pendulum Principle (and Some Basic Training)

THE PRINCIPLE OF THE PENDULUM CAST THAT JOHN HOLDEN developed in England and Ron Arra refined in the United States is similar to that of fly casting, using the momentum of the line (in the case of fly casting) or the sinker to load (bend) the rod. In both fly and surfcasting, the angler maximizes the amount of stored energy in the rod by driving against the momentum of the sinker or line and then releasing it just as the rod starts to unbend.

In a true pendulum cast, the angler swings the sinker in a pendulum motion and then drives against its momentum to load the rod. Speed and strength aren't important here, but smoothness, timing, and practice certainly are, since the key to pendulum casting is moving the arms and the body slowly and in sequence.

All the casts described in this book start out from the same basic position. Imagine that you are standing on the face of a huge clock with the target at 12 o'clock. Position your feet shoulder-width apart with your right foot at 5 o'clock and your left foot at 3 o'clock.

Your reel position should be adjusted so that your hands are also shoulder-width apart with the right thumb on the reel and the left hand on the rod butt. The best way to get this adjustment right is to hold the rod butt under your arm with your elbow slightly bent and reach as far as you can up the rod with your right hand.

You'll need a 30-pound-test shock leader long enough to give you the proper drop (see below) and still wrap around your reel three times. The purpose of this leader is to absorb the shock of the sinker or lure leaving the rod tip at speeds well in excess of 150 MPH. On beaches where there are a lot of rocks or sharp shells, 50-pound-test is a better choice. For most surf fishing situations, 14- to 20-pound test line is adequate. If you're using a heavyweight conventional reel such as the Abu Garcia 7000C3 or the Penn 525 MAG, remember to fill the spool to within an eighth of an inch of the top.

The last and most important step is establishing the proper "drop"—the amount of line between the sinker or lure and the rod tip at the beginning of the cast. As you become more proficient and develop your motor skills, you may want to fine-tune your drop, but a good starting point is to have the sinker even with the first guide, which translates to about seven feet of drop when the rod is held vertically.

The longer the drop, the more time and less effort, and the lighter the sinker will seem because of line stretch. Keep your drop on the short side until you've learned and developed the motor skills and basics, and only then experiment until you find the length that suits you best. If you have problems hitting the ground with the sinker with a seven-foot drop, the rod is probably not moving through the correct arc. Shorten the drop a few inches at a time and see if this helps.

There will be more time to cast with a longer drop because of the wider arc it creates, and a longer drop also allows the sinker to build up more speed. This will make more sense later on when you have mastered the basics of pendulum casting. Theoretically, longer and stiffer rods require longer drops, while shorter and more flexible rods require shorter ones.

Now is probably a good time to go over a few other terms that you'll read a lot in the next few chapters. The two that are the most important—and to some the most perplexing—are the outswing and the inswing, which are the heart of the pendulum cast.

The outswing comes first. Once you've taken the basic casting position, tip the rod slightly to swing the sinker out at about 7 o'clock, taking care that the sinker doesn't swing above the tip of the rod. Nothing to that, right?

Now for the inswing. This is accomplished by picking up the rod with your right hand to swing the sinker back from the apex of the outswing to a position behind and at right angles to the rod. You'll feel a little tug at the rod tip when you've done this correctly.

Another term you'll read a lot is "locked," which simply means that the rod is bent as far as it can possibly bend.

There is no mystery to learning and executing the pendulum cast. There is no age barrier either. All it takes is a little patience and lots of the right kind of practice. The venerable Stan Gibbs took up the pendulum cast in his mid-seventies because it was easier on his body than conventional casting techniques. He was still casting well into his late seventies, so there must be something to it.

Let's talk a little bit about the right kind of practice. Constant practice helps, but constantly practicing poor technique will only produce bad habits and poor casting. The best way to learn is to practice with a partner, even if he or she uses a different style. A partner can observe your cast, compare it with the illustrations in this book, and point out faults.

Executing the field-type pendulum cast with full outswing and inswing is a goal for which every caster can strive, but not on the first day you pick up a rod. No top caster learned his or her style of the pendulum cast all at once. It took most of them many hours over a period of years to build upon the basics and form a good foundation of the proper motor skills.

The modified pendulum cast is capable of producing distances in excess of 525 feet on the practice field when perfected, but it's much safer to practice at the water's edge as long as there is nobody to your right if you're right handed or to your left if you're a southpaw. It also has the advantage of exposing you to actual fishing conditions.

Use a 30- to 50-pound shock leader ahead of a 15- or 17-pound-test running line, depending on the weight of the sinker, for practice. Tie a strong snap to the shock leader, because the greatest wear generally occurs just above the sinker. If you practice on a field, make sure that it is free of other users. Crackoffs have been known to travel 950 feet or more and the sinker leaves the rod tip at speeds of close to 200 MPH. An errant sinker can kill or severely injure an innocent bystander.

No matter what casting technique you use, the direction of the cast will be wild to start with, so bear that in mind when choosing a place to practice. Once you've attained some consistency, you can adjust the position of your feet so that the sinker goes in a safe direction.

No matter what style of the pendulum cast you are learning, the inswing is the most important. Get this wrong and you'll be unable to achieve a fully locked rod. You can practice a proper inswing by dry casting in your backyard. The outswing should be very slow, smooth, and controlled. Try to create a mental picture of being relaxed and floating on a cloud.

Expert casters make the pendulum cast look easy, but don't get discouraged if you can't duplicate their efforts right away. We all were beginners at one time, and the top casters have worked for years to develop their skills. Some people have natural coordination and get good distance with only a few weeks of practice while others are slow learners who often become better casters than the naturals. In either case, there's no substitute for dedication. Keep at it and you may find yourself going beyond your greatest expectations. Good luck!

3

Casting Techniques

OFF-THE-BEACH CAST

We're starting with the off-the-beach cast for several reasons. First, it is the foundation of all the casts mentioned hereafter. It is the cast that should be learned first to develop the casting basics, timing, techniques, and accuracy.

Second, it builds confidence, and third, it is an excellent cast for bait fishing from the beach because it will not throw the bait off the hook since the power increases gradually. The off-the-beach cast uses the resistance of the sand to load the rod when the rig is first pulled off beach. Note Cast is demonstrated with the Lamiglas X RA 132 2 Rod.

Before you start the cast, establish your drop length. It should be from the bottom of the rig to the first collecting guide on the rod. Here, I am taking up a good starting position with my feet shoulder-width apart and the rod placed behind me at a 45-degree angle. With the bait rig or lure lying on the beach at right angles to the rod tip, transfer the body weight to the right leg for takeoff power. The right leg is so very important for power transfer, not only in the off-the-beach cast, but in all the surfcasting techniques in this book.

FOOT POSITIONS FOR CASTING TECHNIQUES

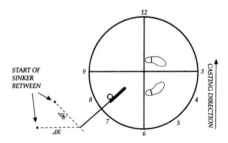

I am starting the cast by pulling the rod through with the whole body and with the left hand controlling the angle of the rod. The rod is starting to preload by lifting the bait rig off the beach. The angler's head is turned to follow the rod through the cast.

The rod is at correct position and my head is up for good balance. The rod is continuing to load. Body weight is beginning to transfer to the left leg with good balance and smooth body motion, and using the whole body.

The rod is in a full locked position with my head upward. The rod is being pulled through the cast with the whole body, and I'm punching up the rod with the right hand and pulling down with the left hand in sequence with the body movement. (Arrow indicates lure.)

The rod is beginning to unload, and the release stage of the cast is taking place. Weight is transferred to the left leg.

The rod is completely unloaded and the cast is released with good accuracy and distance.

The final stage of the cast with complete follow-through with the rod pointed in the direction of the bait rig and line traveling into the air to final touchdown. At night this becomes second nature because of dedication and practice.

THE CANAL CAST

The canal cast doesn't really employ the pendulum principle, but is the most popular cast among surfcasters and handy to know when you're fishing on a crowded beach or have rocks behind you that interfere with a modified pendulum cast. This cast is made almost straight overhead and starts with a much shorter drop than normal, one to two feet of drop depending on how close the structure is behind you.

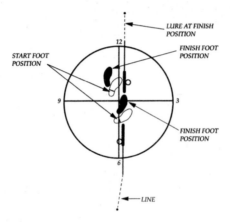

I'm setting up in front of the rocks and as far as possible from the highest obstruction behind me without making contact with the tip of the rod or lure, which is being held higher than normal. Good footing is very important here. Feet should be at shoulder width for good balance.

The outswing should be high enough so the lure will not hit the rocks. My head is turned in the direction of the cast. My weight is transferred to the right leg for power. My knees are bent slightly so the body can turn in a smooth motion.

My head is turned toward the target and the rod is beginning to load with the lure just above the rocks. My weight continues to transfer to my right leg for power.

My head is turned in the direction of my hands and reel. I'm punching upward with my right hand and pulling down with my left hand in smooth, graceful, coordinated motion to create power with little effort.

Rod is being compressed and loaded, and weight is being transferred to the left leg.

Rod is fully locked, and my head is upward and looking at the target. My weight is transferred to my left leg to follow through with the cast, for accuracy.

Final release of locked rod, with my weight on the left leg.

Final stage of cast with rod pointed in the direction of the line and lure to reduce friction. My weight is transferred to both feet for good balance and control.

OVERHEAD BEACH CAST

The overhead beach cast is very similar to the overhead canal cast. The beach cast uses longer drops than the canal cast, and you lean back more at the start of the cast, because you have more room behind you. The overhead beach cast is also made at a slight angle, not directly overhead like the canal cast. It's great to use when there are other surfcasters close by or if you are on a crowded beach.

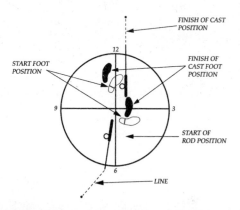

I'm setting up perpendicular to the beach and near the water's edge, holding the rod behind me at an angle. Your knees should be slightly bent for good body movement and balance, which will be used through the entire cast.

(29)

The caster's head is turning with the movement of the rod. Knees are bent and head is up for good balance to start loading the rod by punching upward with the right hand and pulling with the left hand and body. Weight is transferring to the right leg for power.

The body continues to turn toward the water, and the rod tip is lowered to get underneath the rod for more power and compression from body and arms. Note that there is no contact between the line and the beach at any time during the cast.

Body and rod are at the fully loaded, locked position. I'm punching up with the right hand and pulling down with the left hand to create a lever action.

Following through the cast just before final release of the reel spool. Use the whole body in a smooth, graceful movement.

Release of the overhead beach cast, with the rod at the correct angle to follow the lure's direction for good accuracy and distance.

Final follow-through of the cast. Keep the rod tip pointed in the direction of the cast for the final touchdown of the lure.

MODIFIED PENDULUM CAST

This cast is a modified version of the tournament cast that has produced distances of more than eight hundred feet in competition. Nobody's going to get that kind of distance using a one-piece eleven-foot surf fishing rod, but with practice and dedication, anyone can add one hundred feet or more to his or her best distance with a lot less effort than ever before.

The most difficult part of this cast is learning the timing of the outswing and inswing, which will take a little practice, but will never be forgotten once you develop the motor skills. When I first started to learn the pendulum cast I used to go through the motions of the whole cast without using any lure, similar to a baseball player in the on-deck circle before his turn at bat. This method helps a great deal to develop the motor skills needed for the pendulum cast.

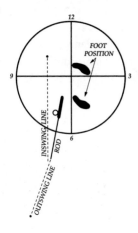

Start of the cast: The position of the rod is almost vertical, tipped slightly to the right so the lure can pass by on the inswing motion. The lure is dropped to the height of the reel, feet are shoulder-width apart, and knees are slightly bent for good balance and control. Head is also slightly up for good balance. If you drop your head and look down you will lose your balance during the cast. If you don't bend your knees slightly you may not be able to turn your body in a smooth, coordinated motion.

The rod is moving the lure to the outswing position by extending the right arm and pulling inward with the left hand. The weight is transferred to the right leg as well.

The lure is at the top of the outswing, but not above the tip of the rod. It's important not to let the lure go above the tip of the rod because you will lose control of the pendulum motion and the lure will not preload the rod. You will feel a slight tug when the lure reaches the apex of just before pulling back on the inswing motion.

The rod is pulled back with the lure moving into the pendulum inswing motion, and will eventually move to the top of the inswing. This motion is done very slowly and gracefully, so do not rush this step.

The lure is in an ideal position behind me at the top of the inswing and at right angles to the rod. Just before the lure reaches its highest point there is a slight pause, and you must start to lean your body and pull the rod through to load it using the whole body and not just the arms.

The rod is beginning to compress and load. Continue to pull the rod throughout the cast, uncoiling your hips and slowly bringing the rod through in a smooth motion, telling yourself not to rush it.

Body twisted towards the water and rod moving into a correct lever position. The body weight is transferring to the left leg for balance and power.

Rod is punched up with the right hand and pulled down with the left hand into the lever position, fully compressed and locked to release the final stages of power to the cast. My weight is also transferred to the left leg.

(3 7)

Final release of the cast with the rod pointed in the direction of the lure to reduce the friction of line traveling through the rod guides. My weight is on my left leg and my head is up for good balance.

Follow the lure as it moves through the air until it touches down. At this point my weight is transferred to both feet.

THE LIGHT TACKLE CAST

Light-tackle surfcasting is done with a surf rod length of seven to nine feet rated for lures of three-eighths of an ounce up to two ounces. Small baitcasting reels and open-face spinning reels are used in light-tackle applications. Light-tackle surf rods can be obtained in one- or two-piece models, rated from 8-pound-test all the way up to 20-pound-test monofilament line. The rod that is being used in the light-tackle photos is the Lamiglas spinning model, XSRA 1083, 9-foot Ron Arra Surf Pro Series rated for $^3/_8$–2 $^1/_4$ oz lures.

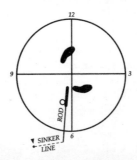

Rod position is in back of you on a slight angle with foot position at shoulder width, twisting at the hips.

Head is focused on the target and rod held behind you above your shoulders, ready to start the cast.

Rod is at fully loaded and locked position with little effort. Start cast by punching upwards with right hand and pulling down with the left hand. Weight is on both feet for good balance. Power comes mostly from upper body and arms, and good rod action. Let the rod do the work.

Release of the cast with little effort. Head up for good balance and rod extended, following lure and line direction, line traveling through guides to final touchdown of lure.

THE WADING PENDULUM CAST

There are places all along the coast where the combination of the deep spot near the beach and an offshore bar make it necessary to wade out as far as possible in order to cast a lure or a bait into the deep water on the far side of the sandbar where the fish are holding. In a situation like this the wading pendulum cast can get you into fish that are out of reach by traditional casting methods.

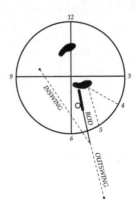

(4 1)

I've waded until I'm knee deep in the water and have established a good, firm foot position. Since I won't be able to move my feet much during the cast, I want to get as much traction as possible, without sinking down into the sand. Feet are placed at shoulder width.

Beginning of the outswing with rod tilted slightly to the right. Lure is dropped down to the first collecting guide.

Lure is swung out in a pendulum fashion to the outswing, by extending the right arm and pulling down with the left hand.

The lure is at the peak of the outswing in ideal position, making sure it is not above the rod tip.

(4 3)

Lure is pulled back by pulling the right arm inward toward the body and pushing the left hand away from the body to start the pendulum inswing.

Body is pivoted to my right and the lure is continuing to move into the pendulum swing.

(4 4)

Rod and lure are towards the water at the end of the inswing. Note that my head has turned and weight is transferring to the right leg, and lure is at correct position, not above rod tip, and at right angles to rod. At this time you will feel a slight tug from the lure moving towards the top of the inswing. This is the time to start the cast, by turning my body to the left and bringing the rod around very slowly and gracefully, with a smooth body motion and in sequence with the arms.

My body is bringing the rod around as my hips start to uncoil. I'm pulling the rod through with my left hand and guiding it with my right. My head is up and my knees are slightly bent for good balance and movement.

The rod is in a fully locked position, ready to release its power. My hands are much higher than normal to keep the lure from hitting the beach or water. I'm punching up with my right hand while pulling down with my left. My body weight is transferring to the left leg and my head is up for good balance and casting accuracy.

The release of the cast. Continue to follow through in a smooth graceful movement. Here I'm keeping the rod lined up with the lure so that the line will follow smoothly through the rod guides.

4

Taking Care of Your Gear and Yourself

I'VE BEEN AN ATHLETE ALL MY LIFE, PLAYING BASEBALL, football, and track in high school and later on professionally in the Pittsburgh Pirates minor league system. The motor skills I developed along the way have undoubtedly helped me become a better caster.

While not every saltwater angler is a pro athlete, there are a few tricks of the athlete's trade that will help improve your distance. One of the most important is warming up before you cast.

I'm not talking about the kind of exercises that you may have seen me go through with wrist weights prior to a Distance Casting competition. You can loosen up just as easily by making twenty-five or thirty dry casts before rigging up your rod, the same way a baseball batter takes practice swings in the on-deck circle while waiting for his turn at the plate. You'll never see a runner, baseball player, or golfer take the field without warming up. Neither should you.

Do your dry casts leisurely—almost in slow motion. The more you cast, the quicker you tend to get, so think slow, right from the start of your warm-ups. Two other good warm-up exercises are trunk twisters and knee lifts. For the latter, lie on your back and punch each

Warm up by making some dry casts while wearing wrist weights. This builds strength and helps increase speed and casting distance.

knee alternately to your chest and hold it there for a three-second count.

Now it's time to turn your attention to your equipment. Before you attach your terminal gear, tie on a big bank sinker and make a couple of casts to stretch out your line and get it nice and wet. Giving the line a good soaking helps get rid of memory coils and eliminates most backlash problems. When you wind the line back on the reel, check to be sure that it's at least an eighth of an inch below the flange of the spool and that the line is coming off the spool on the opposite side from where your right thumb is going to be.

Monofilament line will lose its strength quickly if left exposed to the sun too long. Check and replace line frequently, especially early in the season. Take special care to check the area where your shock leader joins the terminal tackle. That's where the most wear will occur. At the same time, use an old nylon or silk stocking to check your guides for nicks, grooves, or scuffs.

Cleaning and oiling your reels on a regular basis is also critical to distance casting. A good spraying with WD-40 following a tide or two of fishing will do a better job of driving out moisture and grit than a freshwater rinsing. Lubricate regularly, using 3-In-One ten-weight oil in cold weather and 3-In-One twenty-weight when it's hot. Choose the red can for the ten-weight and the blue can for the twenty-weight.

And consider making or purchasing a reel cover. A good surf reel that will get you the distance you want is a major investment and it doesn't have to make many rides down the beach in the back of a 4x4 before the wear and tear starts to show. Even an old sock or a shower cap will provide some protection.

Don't use the outside horizontal or vertical rod holders on your beach buggy or 4x4 until you reach the beach. Investing in a horizontal rod holder that attaches to the ceiling of your vehicle will pay big dividends in preventing damage to your equipment down the road. Take your rods into the shower with you after each session on the beach to get rid of as much salt and sand as possible.

Lures and jigs need care as well. Hooks rust and need constant sharpening, split rings corrode, and soft plastic grubs and skirts often stick to hard plastic plugs. Isolate lures that have been exposed to salt water and give them a good soaking with fresh, soapy water after each outing.

Lures and jigs are a costly investment, so it's well worth the time and trouble to keep them clean, sharp, and in good condition. And a lure that has been allowed to deteriorate from exposure to the harsh saltwater environment could cause you to lose the fish of a lifetime. Keeping your terminal tackle always in good repair will help tilt the odds in your favor when you have a big striper on the business end of your line.

Hooks and knives will stay sharper longer if dipped in lemon juice after sharpening. The acid in the juice leaves a protective coating that rust has difficulty penetrating. Repeat the process after each sharpening.

5

Ten Tips for MoreDistance (and Some Extras)

ISTARTED SURF FISHING AS A TWELVE-YEAR-OLD WITH MY DAD, and I haven't looked back since, but I'm always looking for ways to learn more and improve my technique. That's probably why I got into distance casting to start with. I wondered if it would mean more fish on the beach for me, and it has. It can have the same happy benefits for you.

As we've already demonstrated in previous chapters, brute power is only part of the equation. Timing, smooth coordination of effort, and use of the entire body are also major keys to success. So is the right equipment.

Some of the information in the tips that follow you may have read in earlier chapters, but I am repeating it here for emphasis. These suggestions are not based on tournament casting alone, but from my years of surf fishing experience as well.

----- 1 -----
RODS

Select a rod about ten to eleven feet long with a firm butt section and a fast-action tip that bends in the upper one-third to one-half of the blank. Limber-tipped rods with thin blank walls are designed for freshwater use and are not suited for rough-and-tumble surf fishing. Fiberglass remains a good choice for playing fish and durability with braided lines, but graphite will give you better distance with less effort and excellent bite detection and lure control. It is also lighter in weight. (See list of suppliers in the appendix.)

For conventional casting, I like the reel positioned comfortably at my right arm's length when slightly bent at the elbow. I like a firm butt section, about six BNLG or the new Alconite BMNAG Fuji or NSG silicon carbide guides, with the first gathering guide positioned at least twenty-nine inches ahead of the reel. (On spinning rods make it at least forty inches.)

The first guide should be a #30 followed in order by a #25, #20, #16, #12, #12, #12, and a #12 ring PST silicon carbide Fuji tip-top. Properly aligned, the guides should form a tunnel or cone (see photo). I prefer light guides, which don't distort the action of the blank.

Spinning guides should be GBSVLG Fujis starting with a #40 or #50 BSVLG collecting guide, depending upon the size of the reel

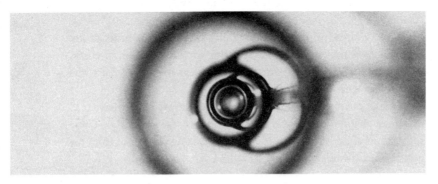

(Patrick Wiseman photo)
When properly aligned, the guides should form a tunnel or cone that will allow the line to pass through with little resistance.

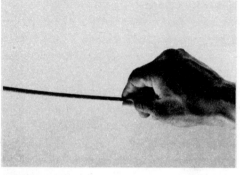

(Patrick Wiseman photo)

Every rod blank has a spine, which will determine proper guide place-ment. I find the spine by resting the upper third of the blank on a chair back or on the edge of a table and rolling it between my thumb and finger-tips. When the blank seems to resist rotation and then jumps ahead, the spine is at the bottom of the blank. Guides on spinning rods should be mounted on the spine, while conventional casting rods work best with the guides mounted directly opposite the spine.

spool. The remaining guides should be Fuji GBSVLGs #30, #20, #16, and #16 capped with a #16 ring BPLT Fuji tip-top.

Whether you build your own rod or have someone else do it for you, make sure that the guides are placed on the opposite side from the spine for a conventional rod and directly on the spine for a spin-ning rod (almost every rod has a spine—the stiff side of the blank). This will increase energy when the rod is loaded and will result in a

(5 3)

longer cast. Bait fishermen may want to put the guides on the spine on conventional rods for more fish-fighting power.

----- 2 -----
REELS

A narrow, light-spooled reel will provided the greatest distance, since there is less friction as the line streams through the first guide. No antibacklash device can replace an educated thumb on the spool's flange, especially when casting against the wind.

When using reels with flanges such as the P220 Newell, 7000 Abu, or Penn 140 Squidder, train your ear as much as your thumb, since a steady spin produces an even, audible whirring sound. Stop the spool the instant the lure splashes down.

A centrifugal brake-block or magnetically controlled reel can help eliminate almost all manual thumbing of the spool to control backlash or overrun. But against the wind, without the educated thumb, you can still create a backlash.

The reel should feature a tough, lightweight spool. We used to worry a lot about fracture under the pressure of memory-banked monofilament, yet this is far less a problem now than it was a couple of decades ago. The new anodized aluminum spools and components absorb a great deal of abuse. Most mistakes now are due to "pilot error," not equipment failure.

---- 3 ----
LINE

Monofilament line outcasts braid, for there is less friction involved in its passage through the guides. Braid offers less stretch and better bite detection, especially when bouncing jigs. The downside to braid is that it has to be spooled under tension to avoid creating backlashes or tangles and is tough on the thumb while retrieving.

Your choice of a suitable line will be a personal matter and it is true that most of the name brands are mighty close in performance. One point should be emphasized: Always purchase a premium grade offered by a recognized firm!

Fill conventional fishing reels to within an eighth of an inch of the spool's rim—not right to the top. Leave space enough to use your thumb in feathering the spool's flange with light pressure. This prevents overrunning of the spool, which causes a backlash.

The secret is to keep the spool running at the same speed as the lure in the air. When fishing, do not completely fill a spinning reel's spool either, for this can lead to some initial tangles. Only tournament casters fill the reel to the top. A spinning reel should never be filled to the top under fishing conditions.

Often, a cast is doomed before launching! It's critical to guide the line onto the spool so that it lies absolutely level. Even slight humps or bumps may slip over onto neighboring coils and may cause the spool to run at different speeds and create either disaster or shortening of the cast. Your left thumb should be "educated" also so that it can level line night or day. No secrets are involved, just a lot of practice.

The lighter the line, the longer the cast will be. Naturally, you will use a shock leader that extends back to several turns around the reel's spool. However, some distance surfcasters tend to forget that in practical fishing one must consider the size of the species sought as well as the bottom structure to contend with. Sometimes it is necessary to sacrifice some distance in order to ensure success.

I do not usually go to ultralight lines on Cape Cod where waters can be turbulent, bass and blues can be record size and one must often contend with rockpiles studded with barnacles. In the Cape Cod Canal, 25- or 30-pound line is a logical choice on a conventional outfit, and often you'll wish you had heavier! Twenty-pound test is about the norm for spinning. On the area's clear sand beaches, one can do very well with 17- or 20-pound on revolving spool, and 14- to 17-pound on spinning tackle. Lighter lines guarantee longer casts, but the angler must be vigilant. Because of the line's smaller diameter, a nick can cause a breakoff and a lost fish, even in the new monofilament lines that test stronger but are thinner in diameter.

----- 4 ------
LURES

Think aerodynamic: We only kid ourselves when we talk about ultimate distance in the surf with anything other than aerodynamic lures. Anything that is wind-resistant will handicap the cast noticeably. The English, who often prefer to use bait instead of lures, have for that reason developed a series of torpedo-shaped sinkers with fold-out grapnel hooks, and they have pioneered clever bottom rigs that keep small baits tucked in against a leader during the cast. Perhaps we go to the other extreme in our preference for artificial lures.

To achieve distance, a plug must be built to cast—or else it will not. The famous Rapala is a fish killer, but too light to achieve any distance. Lots of fine-lipped models are too wind resistant to get way out there. We need something that is admirably streamlined and properly weighted, often at the tail. This may be a popper, swimmer, or other type, depending upon configuration, yet it must be designed to move through the air fluidly.

Certain metal or leadhead jigs are great in the maximum range department, but not all. You get into horizontally flattened models and they tend to plane and sail off course. Best to choose the slim, compact, streamlined models: They'll shoot straight toward a far horizon. Many leadhead jigs are excellent casters and can be deadly when thrown into the edge of a boiling rip.

--------------- 5 ---------------
BODY MOTION

Get your whole body into it. When casting, don't rely on arms and shoulders alone: Use leg and hip movement to generate maximum power. Your entire body should cooperate, and the movement should be well-timed and smooth. I have often likened this to the swing of a great hitter in baseball—fluid motion.

The true pendulum cast will attain greatest distance, yet it must often be varied to suit local conditions. Personally, even from an uncluttered high and dry position, I like to keep my layback somewhat higher than most surfcasters advocate if the beach is not rubbled or if I am not working from a rockpile.

It's important to maintain balance and keep your head up. Think always of smooth, coordinated power, since the jerky, half-interrupted swing invariably produces a backlash or a short throw. Strive to be "smooth as silk." That's one of the big secrets.

----- 6 -----
WIND

Under adverse conditions against the wind, level out each cast to keep the trajectory low—since in windy conditions a high cast will result in hampering wind resistance and bellying of the following line. Conversely, when the wind is at your back it can be an advantage to throw high and let Mother Nature help.

---------- 7 ----------
ACCURACY

Accuracy is important. At short range it becomes relatively easy to master, but at 100 yards and beyond there can be difficulty in pinpointing a target. The solution lies in constant practice: After a while the close shot becomes almost instinctive. A highly efficient surfman is very likely to touch down in something like a ten-foot circle at one hundred yards or more.

---------- 8 ----------
WEATHER

Accept the Weather: Wind, weather, and surf conditions may help or hurt. There's no way you'll achieve eye-popping range with a gale-force wind in your teeth, so accept that. If it seems necessary to wade, heavy surf will knock you off balance. However, under such inclement conditions, a good caster will still reach further than a neighbor who has not practiced the art. Lucky for us, many fish are apt to move closer to shore during a blow or at night.

---------------- 9 ----------------
NIGHT FISHING

I see no major difference between night and day surfcasting. Techniques are precisely the same—if a bit more meticulous—after dark. The spinning outfit certainly is easiest to use at night, but anyone who has mastered the revolving spool will find that casting becomes almost instinctive. The line is laid properly by that educated thumb, and the whole operation becomes more feel than vision. On the darkest of nights you can hedge your bets by wearing a small penlight on a cord around your neck to illuminate the reel while retrieving.

--------- 10 ---------
PRACTICE

Practice! Maybe this sounds obvious, yet it is one of the keys to success. Visit the fishing grounds whenever you can, but practice good techniques in all seasons. There are folks who make snide remarks when they see casters throwing unarmed weights on football fields or deserted beaches during the chill winter months, conveniently forgetting that these enthusiasts are honing their skills.

There is no quick and easy road to success: Indeed it takes hard work. It took me ten years before I thought I was ready for tournament competition, yet it surely paid off.

But more important than that, I'm a better fisherman through an appreciation of tackle and a better understanding of techniques. You can be, too.

EXTRA TIPS

Rinse your reels lightly with fresh water after each trip, being careful not to drive the salt into the gears. Spray with WD-40 to drive out moisture, then lightly oil all components.

Leave a scant side play on conventional reels—just enough so that you can almost not feel anything at all. This will increase distance at the final stages of touchdown.

Stick with low-profile conventional reels if you have a choice. Your thumb will slip less and you'll have better control of the spool and achieve more distance.

Tying on the right shock leader is important, especially if you're casting for distance. The formula is simple: Just multiply the weight of the lure or sinker by ten.

For example, with a three-ounce lure, multiply by ten and tie on a 30-pound-test leader; for a five-ounce sinker a 50-pound-test leader should be used. I personally use a leader that is twice the length of the rod I'm using, especially where there is lots of structure such as barnacles, rocks, boulders, ledges, and drop-offs.

6

Rigging for That Faraway Fish

A S WE POINTED OUT IN THE INTRODUCTION, THIS BOOK IS about long-distance fishing, not long-distance casting. The modified pendulum cast wasn't developed to win distance-casting titles; it was developed because striped bass were feeding in the middle of the Cape Cod Canal and outside the Sandwich Bar and there was no other way to reach them. That was very frustrating to me.

Obviously you're not going to be able to throw a gob of clams with a heavy pyramid sinker on a fish-finder rig four or five hundred feet and have it arrive in one piece. But there are some bait rigs that work better than others, some of which are illustrated here.

Most of the long-distance fishing done in the United States is done with jigs or lures, the more aerodynamic in design the better. I like to tie them right to the shock leader with a Palomar knot or use a single snap without a swivel. I find that this gives the lure a better action.

When I'm jigging bucktails for striped bass in the Cape Cod Canal, which has some vicious currents that can tangle lines, I'll tie on a barrel swivel about three feet ahead of the jig using 40- or fifty-pound-test mono tied to the barrel swivel with braided line ahead of the jig as the main line. If you do this, make sure to use a barrel swivel of eighty to one hundred-pound test.

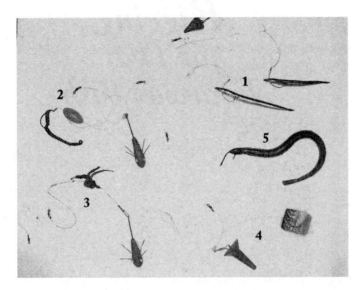

Five basic bait rigs that work. Clockwise from upper left:

1. High-low bottom-fishing rig with sand eels on two wide-gap #5/0 hooks. Note that each hook is placed into the top of the sand eel's head first, then into the body.

2. Float rig with sea worm using an offset-shank #4/0 Gamakatsu worm hook. A popular variation involves replacing the float with a floating Rapala plug with hooks and split rings removed, mounted so the Rapala hangs upside down.

3. Long-range, distance-casting bottom rig with a sea worm. Note: Before casting attach the hook to the shield snugly towards the sinker so both leaders are straight. This helps prevent the bait from flying off and allows you to cast farther.

4. Chunk bait rig with a fish-finder and a mackerel chunk on a #7/0 Gamakatsu Octopus hook.

5. Live eel rig with a #5/0 Gamakatsu Octopus hook placed through the underside of the eel's jaw and then up through the eye. This allows the rig to be cast and retrieved slowly to attract striped bass.

I normally use 20- to 30-pound-test mono running line behind my 50-pound shock leader. The best way to connect the two is to tie an overhand knot in the shock leader, run the lighter line through, and tie a Uni knot with the lighter line around the shock leader. Wet both lines and pull the knots until they tighten and butt up against one another. This makes a nice, compact connection that slides through the guides easily.

Top to bottom: Gag's grabber Bluefish Bomb, 1.7 ounce. Good for surface-feeding fish, this one can be retrieved fast or slowly. Casts very well for a lightweight surface lure.

A 2-ounce Atom popper with a ⅜-ounce bucktail jig. This is a light lure good for rough water, and should be retrieved slowly.

English-style Baitsafe lure, 4 ounces, used as a bottom rig, with sea worms. The lure hits the water and opens up to let the bait fall out.

Atom Ketch 'n Fetch, 3 ounces, with a 3-ounce leadhead bucktail jig.

Super Strike Bullet, 1⅝ ounces. Good for reaching beyond the sandbars at daylight to find feeding fish.

(63)

Top to bottom: Stan Gibbs 3¼-ounce Polaris Popper, excellent for feeding stripers at daybreak. Casts like a rocket.

Roberts lure, 4 ounces. One of my favorite bluefish lures.

Atom popper, Swingin' Swiper, 2 ounces. Great for both stripers and bluefish. The single hooks aids in catch-and-release.

Stan Gibbs Pencil Popper, 3 ounces. Good all-around surface lure that does well in fast-moving water. Best at daybreak and just before dark.

Creek Chub popper, 2⅛ ounces. Another good all-around surface lure, this one makes noisy pops to attract feeding fish.

Clockwise from upper left: Bomber swimmer, 7 inches and 1½ ounces, with an Eddystone Eel dropper. I've caught hundreds of striped bass with this lure, most of them at night. It casts very well for a lightweight lure.

Super Strike Little Neck Popper. Best at early morning and before dark, this one casts well with little effort.

Roberts lure, 4 ounces with a bucktail streamer. Great for casting into the wind.

Reverse Atom lure, 3½ ounces. Great when fish are feeding on squid, this can be used night or day.

Stan Gibbs Skipper, 2¼ ounces. Aerodynamically shaped for excellent casting. Works well in fast-moving water.

Stan Gibbs Swimmer, 3 ounces. Very good for large fish or when fish are feeding on big baitfish such as porgies or menhaden.

Atom Ketch 'n Fetch, 3 ounces.

Top to bottom: Single-hook eelskin rig, 3½ ounces. Best when cast upcurrent and bounced along the bottom. Pork rind can be added to the hook.

Shorty Hopkins lure, 2¼ ounces. Can be used any time of day, though I usually choose this one when the weather is rough.

A 4½-ounce Hopkins with a ⅜-ounce bucktail jig.

Bill Upperman jig, 2 ounces. This works well with pork rind on the hook. This bucktail will catch any species of fish, and the US Navy includes it in survival kits!

Leadhead bucktail jig, 5 ounces. A great casting lure, this can be used with pork rind on the hook. Good for fast currents.

Leadhead bucktail, 3 ounces.

Super Strike Needle Fish, 1¾ ounces. Good at night and in swiftmoving water. Should be retrieved very slowly.

FILLING A REVOLVING-SPOOL REEL

Insert a pencil into the supply spool to allow the fishing line to feed smoothly off the spool. Have someone hold each end of the pencil while you turn the reel handle. Keep proper tension on the line by having the person holding the pencil exert a slight inward pressure on the supply spool. *Courtesy DuPont Stren.*

NOTE: keep line level when retrieving line.

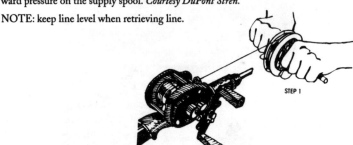

FILLING A SPINNING REEL

You fill a spinning/open-face reel differently than a bait-casting reel because you must allow for the rotation of the pick-up bail which may cause the line to twist. Follow these steps:

1. Have someone hold the supply spool or place it on the floor or ground.
2. Pull the line so that it spirals (balloons) off the end of the spool.
3. Thread the line through the rod guides and tie the line to the reel with the bail in the open position. Hold the rod tip three to four feet away from the supply spool. Make fifteen to twenty turns on the reel handle, then stop.
4. Check for line twist by moving the rod tip to about one foot from the supply spool. If the slack line twists, turn the supply spool completely around. This will eliminate most of the twist as you wind the rest of the line onto the reel.
5. Always keep a light tension on fishing line when spooling any reel. Do this by holding the line between the thumb and forefinger of your free hand.

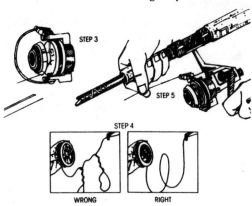

ALBRIGHT SPECIAL

I use the Albright for tying a leader to a lighter main line and for tying mono to wire. When you need a strong knot, this is the best. *Courtesy DuPont Stren.*

1. Double back a couple inches of the heavy line and insert about 10 inches of the light line through the loop in the heavy line.

2. Wrap the light line back over itself and over both strands of the heavy line. While doing this you are gripping the light line and both leader strands with the thumb and finger of your left hand, and winding with your right.

3. Make ten turns, then insert the end of the line back through the loop once more at the point of original entry.

4. Pull gently on both ends of heavy line sliding knot toward loop. Remove slack by pulling on standing and tag ends of light line. Pull both standing lines as tight as possible and clip off excess from both tag ends.

JOINING LINES

1. Overlap ends of two lines of about the same diameter for about 6 inches. With one end, form Uni-Knot circle, crossing the two lines about midway of overlapped distance.

2. Tie basic Uni-Knot, making six turns around the two lines.

3. Pull tag end to snug know tight around line.

4. Use loose end of overlapped line to tie another Uni-Knot and snug up.

5. Pull the two standing lines in opposite directions to slide knots together. Pull as tight as possible and snip ends close to nearest coil.

PALOMAR KNOT

This is my favorite knot for large hook eyes, sinker eyes, and tournament sinker connections. *Courtesy DuPont Stren.*

1. Double about 4 inches of line and pass loop through eye.

2. Let hook hang loose and tie overhand knot in doubled line. Avoid twisting the lines and don't tighten.

3. Pull loop of line far enough to pass it over hook, swivel or lure. Make sure loop passes completely over this attachement.

4. Pull both tag end and standing line to tighten. Clip tag end.

This knot is equally as good as the Improved Clinch for terminal tackle connections and is easier to tie, except when using large plugs. It, too, is used by most of the pros.

IMPROVED CLINCH KNOT

I use this knot for small hook eyes, lure eyes, and swivels. It's quick and simple to tie. *Courtesy DuPont Stren.*

This is a good knot for making terminal-tackle connections and is best used for lines up to 20-pound test. It is a preferred knot by professional fishermen and angling authorities.

1. Pass line through eye of hook, swivel, or lure. Double back and make five turns around the standing line. Hold coils in place; thread end of line around first loop above the eye, then through big loop as shown.

2. Hold tag end and standing line while coils are pulled up. Take care that coils are in spiral, not lapping over each other. Slide tight against eye. Clip tag end.

(69)

TOURNAMENT CASTING KNOT

Another variation on the Uni-knot, this one employs a burr melted onto the tip of the shock leader to prevent the smaller-diameter main line from slipping. Keep this burr as small as possible to minimize the friction as it moves through the guides.

If you are connecting very light mono-filament to a heavy leader, use a match or cigarette lighter to create a burr on the tag end of the heavy leader. Keep the burr small, but bulky enough to prevent the light line from slipping over it.

1. Overlap ends of two lines of about the same diameter for about 6 inches. With one end, form Uni-Knot circle, crossing the two lines about midway of overlapped distance.

30- TO 60-POUND TEST SHOCK LEADER

12- TO 17-POUND TEST MAIN LINE

2. Tie basic Uni-Knot, making six turns around the two lines.

PULL AND SLIDE TO BUMP AGAINST BURR

SNIP TO 1/32"

7

*L*ong-Distance Fishing

O NCE YOU'VE GOTTEN THE LURE WHERE YOU WANT IT, long-distance casting gives way to long-distance fishing. Remember that you've got three hundred or four hundred feet of stretchy monofilament between you and your lure or bait. It's important to keep a fairly tight line in order to be able to feel a strike.

And when you do feel that hit, don't try to set the hook. Even with a tight line there will be too much stretch to do that effectively. Wait until the fish has hooked itself and started to take line. And it goes without saying that your hooks should be sharp enough to catch on your thumbnail! Many surf veterans have switched to circle hooks because the fish tend to hook themselves in the corner of the jaw.

Okay, you've delivered the goods, the fish has hit, and there is thirty pounds of unhappy striped bass firmly on the end of your line. Now what?

This depends upon what conditions you've got to deal with. Playing a fish in the Cape Cod Canal, where the water is constantly moving, is a different ball game from the Sandwich Bar or the beaches at

Sandy Neck. Having some kind of idea of the conditions ahead of time can prevent a lot of heartache later on.

For instance, are there other anglers nearby? Are they baitfishing or throwing plugs? What's going to happen when somebody gets a fish on? Often it's wise to walk over and agree on a game plan just in case a fish starts to run along the beach or up and down the Canal. In the process, keep an eye open for mussel beds or open areas of beach that may be helpful later in the process of landing a fish.

The biggest mistake most anglers make is to apply too much drag and pressure too soon after setting the hook. Too much pressure often prompts the striper to sound deep into the structure below and become very difficult to turn or move with any style of surf rod and line.

If this happens, lighten the drag and let the fish run. Most will eventually come towards the surface for easier playing. Another method that often works when the fish can't be moved is to twang the line as if it were a guitar string. This sends vibrations to the fish that it does not like.

Always play a fish with an even drag setting that is not too tight or too light and adjust according to size of fish and speed of current. Let your fish run and tire before attempting to gain back line. One of the biggest complaints I hear is that the new graphite surf rods cast great but will not play a fish properly. The people who are complaining tend to try to horse their fish in and often end up tearing the hook from the fish's mouth.

The true tournament distance-casting rod does not flex enough, especially in the butt section, to play a fish correctly, especially a running striper.

Most tournament rods are twelve to fourteen feet long and their length is not needed. The ideal fishing rod should have a firm butt section that will flex and tire a fish instead of pulling the hooks out of its mouth. A length of nine feet, six inches to eleven feet is just right for playing stripers or blues.

There have been many forty-pound-plus stripers caught with nine-foot fly rods on the beach, so why not with a ten- or eleven-foot graphite surf rod? The proper angle of the surf rod—about forty-five degrees—is imperative. This creates good leverage on the fish and more fun for the fisherman.

"High-sticking,"—raising the rod to the vertical position—creates no leverage on a fish, but it does definitely break many graphite surf rods. Most times fish will sound deep and shake off. If the rod is held too high you will only use the tip section of the rod and never be able to create the necessary leverage. Yes, it's happened to me more times than I care to count.

Let other nearby anglers know when you've got a fish on and tell them what you're going to try to do. Remember, take your time and tire your fish and play the surf, waves, and shallow mussel beds to your advantage. If you can get the fish into shallow water, beaching it is seldom a problem. If the fish is bigger and won't come in, tire it out and then take advantage of each big wave to "surf" it a little closer, using a pumping action of your rod to lever it into shallow water, or, in the case of the Cape Cod Canal, onto a convenient mussel bed.

On the beach where there is lots of surf, waves are an important factor and must be played correctly when your fish is close to shore. Concentrate on feeling the push and pull of the waves and undertow,

Take your time playing the fish. Keeping the rod at the proper angle is also very important.

which will pull your fish away from you quickly just when you thought you had him in. Be ready to let the spool go if the fish does not want to go your way. Wait for another good wave that is pushing towards the beach and try again.

Look for shallow areas to fish where the drop-offs are gradual and not severe. You will land more fish!

Sometimes a mussel bed can be an angler's best friend. This one certainly helped me land this Cape Cod Canal striper.

I always remember my dad's advice, especially when I was trying to beach my first striper on Sandy Neck. He cautioned me to hold the rod up at a forty-five-degree angle and play the fish with a light but firm drag, letting the fish run and tire itself out before reeling in.

Dad coached me to use a pumping technique by dropping the tip slightly while retrieving, pulling up on the rod without reeling, and repeating the process by lowering the tip again and reeling in. This method is less tiring and there is less chance of pulling the hook from the fish's mouth, but is not recommended for soft-mouthed species such as weakfish and haddock.

Instead of using a hand gaff, the BogaGrip or gripper tool is a safer way to grab a fish by the lip and also catch and release correctly.

Keep in mind once the fish is on the beach that most species have teeth and aren't bashful about using them, so don't try grabbing them by the lips. A safer approach is to grab the fish by the neck of its tail with some beach sand in your hand so your grip will not slip when grabbing the fish by the neck of its tail and get it into a cooler as soon as possible.

Landing a striper at the Cape Cod Canal.

8

Start Youngsters Off Right

ANYBODY WHO HAS FISHED A TIDE OR TWO AND WATCHED the sun come boiling out of Cape Cod Bay on a midsummer's morning will remember that first fishing trip as if it were yesterday. For me it was a trip to Sandy Neck Beach on Cape Cod with my dad and his good fishing buddy, Jack Kelly. I was all of twelve years old.

We drove down to the Neck from Needham, where dad was a firefighter for thirty-three years. Our "beach buggy" was Kelly's battered Jeep Wagoneer, and catching striped bass and bluefish from the beach was dad's passion. He was hoping that it would be my passion too, and was taking every step he could on this trip to make me a participant instead of just an observer.

The first thing we had to do was let air out of the tires down to twelve pounds so we would not bog down in the soft sand while traveling on the beach. I helped in this task and was told to count to a certain number and they would take over the task of letting air out to the proper pressure with their tire gauge.

Once the pressure was established we were on our way to the beach trail along the Great Marsh, which is the backside of Sandy

Neck beach. Soon we were approaching the beautiful tall white sand dunes and turning off onto a deep sandy trail that eventually led to the front beach trail which was better to drive on.

My dad and his friend were still telling their fish tales while driving. We finally arrived where there were lots of seagulls sitting on the sand at the water's edge. This was the spot. "Look at the birds," said Dad as Kelly parked the Wagoneer at the high water mark. "They wouldn't be here if there hadn't been some feeding action recently."

There was only one other beach buggy in the distance with surf rods out bottom fishing. It was about 4 AM, still dark, about dead low tide. It was my time to learn, being my first trip surf fishing on the beach. It was time for me to help unload the gear. Rods, sand spikes, bait, and lantern were set out a little ways from the water's edge.

I was shown how to rig up and place the sand spikes so they would be secure enough for a big hit from a bass. There were four rods that were rigged up with sea worms and cut mackerel. The worms had float rigs and the cut bait had a standard fish-finder rig with no float.

My dad and Kelly showed me how to sharpen and bait the hook and put the pyramid sinker onto the fish-finder. We were ready to fish between two sandbars with the tide already coming in. My dad walked onto the sandbar and made a cast with his Penn 140 reel. In the dark, I could hear the noise of the spool running and stopping. We walked back up the beach together, placed the surf rod into the sand spike, set the clicker on the reel, and set a light drag. Kelly did the same thing as my dad but used sea worms instead of cut mackerel.

Now it was a waiting game, sitting on the beach listening to the old men tell more fish tales. The tide was down and there was a clean beautiful sweet smell from the ocean and of the Great Marsh behind us. It was fall but not cold enough for me to go back into the Wagoneer. This was a new adventure that would change my life forever.

I heard them say that they would fish here at this spot until one hour outgoing, meaning that one hour after high tide we would move to a different spot if we had no luck here. We moved our sand spikes back as the tide moved toward us.

At this time the water was almost up to the top of the sandbar, and I heard a reel scream and saw the rod tip bending towards the water. My dad picked it up quickly, took the clicker off, dropped the

My dad, Ray Arra Sr. and me in 1985 at the DuPont Stren New England Surfcasting Championships in Falmouth, Massachusetts. At this event I broke the US record with a cast of 737 feet, 11 inches and became the first American to cast beyond 700 feet using 0.35mm line.

Dad introduced me to surfcasting when I was twelve years old, and I have never forgotten the valuable techniques he taught me. He recently passed away at age 81.

tip, and free-spooled the fish until it slowed down. Once he had set the hook and made sure the fish was on well, he handed me the rod and told me to play the fish against the drag of the reel.

What a feeling! Dad told me to hold the rod up at an angle of about forty-five degrees, playing the fish with a light but firm drag, letting the fish run and tire itself out before reeling in.

I did what I was told to do because I didn't want to lose that fish. Dad coached me to use a pumping technique, dropping the tip slightly when retrieving, pulling up on the rod without reeling, and repeating the process by lowering the tip again and reeling in. This method is less tiring and there is less chance of pulling the hook from the fish's mouth, but it is not recommended for soft-mouthed species such as weakfish and haddock.

It was hard for me to relax at this exciting time, but I managed to play the fish for about fifteen minutes—which felt more like an hour—with a lot of help from my dad. I finally backpedaled, beached the fish, and carefully removed the hooks with pliers. Kelly ran over with the sun just starting to rise in the distance off the water. I was thrilled. More than that, I was hooked!

Dad measured the striper. It was thirty-nine inches long and weighed about twenty pounds. I wanted to catch my next fish on my own but unfortunately this was the only fish we caught through the whole tide.

Over the years, dad and I sampled a great deal of fresh- and saltwater fishing and upland hunting, and studied wildlife habits, but that first striper was something special. After this trip I knew I wanted to be on Cape Cod someday, and did finally move to the Sandy Neck Road in 1977.

There was a lot to learn, but Dad was always there to help. As a young boy I learned to cast with a conventional Penn Surfmaster reel mounted on an eight-foot surf rod built on a slow-action blank that curved progressively through the entire length of the rod. Dad picked it out, saying it would give me a good feel and help me to learn the basics of casting.

The reel had no braking system or level-wind mechanism, but it did have a good thumb flange to control the spool during the cast so it would not backlash.

When starting out I had lots of backlashes and tangles, especially when using the 36-pound braided squidding line that was popular in those days. Squidding line had to be retrieved just right so it was level and tight on the spool before casting.

I would cast two- to three-ounce pencil poppers to practice accuracy and distance. Later on I went to spinning tackle when I had saved enough money, buying a Garcia nine foot, medium-heavy action, two-piece rod with metal ferrules. The matching reel was a model 302 Garcia spinning reel filled with 17-pound-test mono tied directly to the lures my dad made from broomstick handles.

Selecting the right equipment can often make the difference between hooking a youngster on fishing or turning him off. The ideal setup for a twelve-year-old starting out today is a graphite or fiberglass spinning rod of eight-and-a-half or nine feet depending of the size and strength of the child. The rod should be a slow-action model that curves progressively through the entire length of the blank. This slow action will load and bend easily and cast with little effort to achieve good distance and fish-fighting abilities.

When the youngster gets older and stronger, graduate to a nine- to ten-foot, moderate-action rod that curves in the upper half of the rod. This rod will have more power in the butt section to transfer the power from the cast to the tip for longer casts and better lure control and fish-fighting abilities.

The spinning outfit is the best choice for the novice, offering fewer tangles and more ease of use with no backlashes. The conventional reel with its revolving spool takes longer to master.

The conventional reel does have its advantages, as it will handle heavier line without losing distance, and provides better bite detection. Conventional reels also sport better drag systems and more casting distance (20 percent more than spinning).

If a youngster wants to advance in surfcasting, becoming familiar with a conventional, revolving-spool outfit will pay off later on. My first choice of reel would be the Penn Model 710Z open-face Spinfisher Series with a 3.6:1 retrieve or the 706Z that has a retrieve of 3.8:1 and will hold more line and stand up under heavy-duty use. Both reels hold enough line to handle a big striper. They are excellent starter reels for the beginning surfcaster and are reasonably priced.

Much of the fun of fishing comes from building and fishing your own rigs and lures. My dad taught me how to tie and assemble my own bottom rigs to cut down the cost of buying them all made up. We made bottom rigs using a sliding fish-finder which slides against a single barrel swivel and heavy leader material tied directly to the hook, and a sinker attached to the fish-finder.

I caught a lot of stripers using surface poppers made by my dad, turned down from old broomstick handles and painted blue and white, with screw eyes holding a treble hook in the center and another treble with bucktail for the tail hook.

I caught my first striper all by myself using this outfit. I was at World's End in Hingham, Massachusetts. Dad and I fished there many times and caught fish almost every time, using only surface poppers.

The first striper I caught on my own was something I will never forget because of the tremendous hit and splash that came out of nowhere. Poppers are still my favorite way to catch stripers, bluefish, or any sportfish. World's End was close to home, and we would make sure to be there at low tide to walk out to the mussel bed at the point and fish the incoming tide in the early morning.

A word about technique. It's part of the puzzle like everything else, and without it, you're likely to go fishless. For instance, at World's End casting upcurrent works the best, because it covers more area and the lure can then move on its own buoyancy with the current to enter rips where the stripers are. It is very important to let the lure move with the current and not retrieve it across current.

When you work the lure across the current you're pulling the lure away from the fish most of the time. Instead, give the surface lure a slow action by popping the lure to make it look like the real thing.

One thing I can't emphasize enough is that the best equipment you can buy isn't going to turn a kid on to fishing unless he or she catches fish. A great place to start is a beach, dock, or jetty where many different species of game fish and bottom dwellers hang out. Remember it's quantity and not quality that counts with youngsters. The trophy fish will come later.

9

The
Two-Handed
Fly Rod
Finds a Home

REGULARS FISHING THE BANKS OF THE CAPE COD CANAL OVER
the past few years have reported newcomers in their midst.
Thanks to innovations from manufacturers in several countries, including Lamiglas right here in the US, fly casters are joining the fun.

The fly rods these newcomers are using to stalk the riprap and jet-
ties for cruising striped bass and other gamesters are like nothing
ever seen before along the Ditch. They're fifteen feet long with grips
fore and aft of the reel seat and are meant to be used with two hands.
And they'll throw a fly amazing distances, compared to standard
one-handed models.

Long, two-handed Spey rods are no strangers to anyone who has
fished the rivers of Scotland where having room for an adequate
backcast is a rare experience indeed, but these new English-style
two-handers are a horse of a different color. They lack the limber,
slow action that allows the Spey caster to throw a roll cast without
getting impossibly tangled in shoreline brush behind him, in favor of
a firm butt section that allows remarkably long deliveries.

Commonly referred to as salmon rods, the English models are becoming increasingly popular with steelhead anglers in the Northwest, and they're rapidly building a loyal following among saltwater anglers for their ability to throw a long line and keep it up out of the surf. When there is room behind me, I've thrown much further casts with less effort than when using a nine-foot, one-handed model.

Most salmon rods such as the Lamiglas TM1510 fifteen-foot graphite model are 10 or 11 weight and designed primarily for roll casting, a handy feature along the Canal's brushy shoreline. They're also handy in controlling a fly or streamer in the Ditch's tricky currents. It should be noted that the British and Europeans are rapidly becoming fans of the new steelhead models as they emphasize casting performance over fish-fighting potential.

These new rods are more of a revival than a new idea. Our European brethren have been using them for years because they can catch more fish with them. Europeans fish salmon for nine months of the year and tend to keep their catch. Americans may get in two weeks of salmon fishing a year and don't consider a two-hander worth the investment.

But that was before somebody had the bright idea of taking on salt water. Venues like the Canal in Massachusetts and Louisiana's bayou country are loaded with gamefish that can be reached by anyone with the equipment and skill to throw a long line.

The new two-handers have a distinctive American touch. Thanks to the latest innovations in graphite, they're light and easy to use, and the potential to catch more fish in salt water makes them well worth the investment.

The two-handed rod isn't ideal for all surf fly-fishing conditions, but it has its moments, and fishing the Canal is one of them. No matter what the application, a large-capacity fly reel with a good anti-reverse or direct-drive drag and a weight-forward line backed by 20-pound-test Dacron is a necessity.

The main difference between a two-handed fly rod and a one-handed model is that you're using both hands to cast the fly. The left hand does most of the work if you employ good rod motion, with the right hand controlling the line.

Most newcomers to the two-hander do not realize just how long the rod really is. They need to realize that the tip is travelling in a

The correct hand position for a two-handed fly rod, with the line held under the middle finger of the right hand. A stripping basket makes casting easier.

much wider arc which produces the longer distance. The size of the loop in the line—which dictates the distance of the cast—is determined by the distance this very long rod moves between the start and stop positions of the cast.

In most cases, a weight-forward line is best fished with a long leader for shallow fish. For bottom feeders such as redfish, flounder, fluke, sea bass, and other species, use a sink-tip line with a very short leader (four feet) to keep the fly on the bottom.

My favorite line for my two-handed fifteen-foot Lamiglas three-piece is the WindCutter interchangeable-tip Spey line pioneered and developed by Jim Vincent of RIO Products. This fly line has many positive features for saltwater fishing, including great casting distance potential and ease of control.

RIO manufactures one-piece floating lines and floating running lines with versatile interchangeable-tip Spey lines for different saltwater fly-casting situations. The WindCutter comes in three sections. It happens to be my favorite because it casts a great distance with little effort and you do not need any extra spools or reels. The first section of fly line is the running line that is attached to the fly line backing and tapers to a thicker body with a loop at the end so the second section of fly line can be attached with a loop-to-loop connection.

This tapered middle section has a loop on each end so it may be attached in turn to a floating- or sinking-tip that is also fitted with a loop. What's unique about this line is that it casts very large flies with little effort and performs as well or better than a one-piece fly line.

The fly line loops are tied so as not to cause any "hinge" effect when attached for excellent casting and multiple applications.

This is the best line for learning the roll cast or Spey cast as well as for sinking-tip fishing. The middle section and floating tip can be removed, allowing attachment of a RIO density-compensated twenty-four-foot sinking-tip head directly to the belly. This enables you to get the fly very deep while controlling its drift and swing with the floating section.

Throwing a fly line long enough to reach striped bass cruising the riprap of the Canal or lurking along an offshore bar isn't as difficult as it looks. Here's how it's done:

THE ROLL CAST

My rod is extended parallel to the water and my weight is on the left foot. If right-handed, the left foot is forward of the right foot in a well-balanced, comfortable position. Keep your head up at a slight angle, the same as you would do for surfcasting. This will help you keep your balance.

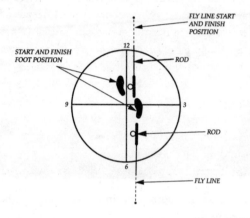

Rod is being raised by pulling up with right hand and pushing down with left hand.

Rod is being raised into correct position. My weight is being transferred to my right foot.

Rod is pulled back high to the correct position between 1 and 2 o'clock to start the roll cast by pulling left hand towards body.

Rod is being loaded by accelerating forward with right hand and pulling down with left, and weight is transferred to the left foot.

Rod is unloading as I've stopped the rod to create the forward loop in the line needed for a good roll cast.

Rod is extended and unloaded, and fly line is released from the right middle finger. My weight is now on my left foot.

Rod is held high at correct angle. My head is up and my weight is transferred to both feet for good balance and finish of roll cast.

THE BACKCAST

Rod is held off the water in an extended right arm position with left foot in front of right foot at shoulder width, for good balance.

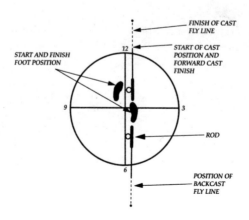

Weight is transferring to right leg and rod is being pulled back upward with the right hand, and the left hand is pulling down, doing most of the work with very little effort.

Weight is transferred to the right leg and rod is pulled back with a smooth, gentle motion with the left hand doing most of the work.

Rod is pulled back in a smooth motion and stopped at 1 o'clock, letting the fly line extend back behind you before starting the forward cast. The size of the loop in the fly line is determined by the distance between where you start and stop the cast, so be careful not to let the rod dip behind you too much.

Forward cast position in a smooth, graceful motion, letting the rod, body, and hands do the work for you.

Right arm is fully extended with the left hand pulled against the chest, stopping the rod to unload and to propel the fly line.

Release of the line and rod in finish cast position parallel to the water, with fly line shooting out toward the water.

Two-handed fly rods allow you to cast big flies like these, designed to imitate large baitfish.

10

Stan Gibbs:
Still the Master

STAN GIBBS MADE HIS FIRST LURES BY HAND IN 1945. THEY worked so well on Cape Cod's Canal and beaches that, in 1946, he was forced to turn to a lathe in order to keep up with demand. About four hundred lures were made that year and sold so quickly that some of them left his shop with the paint still tacky. In 1947, a thousand lures where made and sold.

In those early days there was no tank testing. Stan would travel along a path from the back of his house to the Cape Cod Canal three or four times a day to test his lures so they would cast well and have the action he wanted.

Stan Gibbs turned eighty-six in 2001, and is a true surfcasting legend. He is one of the few who made a living at it. He was an excellent help to me as a new resident of Cape Cod, and was a great mentor when I was learning the Cape beaches and the Cape Cod Canal.

Stan became one of my disciples of sorts when he took up pendulum casting in his late seventies. He didn't do it for the distance, he said, he did it because it was easier on his body. Pendulum casting is just the thing for women and youngsters as well, for the same reasons.

Master luremaker Stan Gibbs on the beach, about 1951.
(photo courtesy Bill Chapin collection)

Having sold his business some years ago, Stan Gibbs is now handcrafting fish as a sculptor. Drawing on his many years of experience, Stan carves fish the way he sees them, painstakingly complete in every detail, just as he did when making his lures more than a half century ago.

Many of Stan's lure creations have found their way into the collection of angler and lure collector Edward Poore of Sagamore, Massachusetts. These lures are a small part of Ed's collection of more than two hundred early examples of New England area surf-fishing lures made for striped bass fishing.

Most of these early lures were designed to imitate the whiting, a baitfish abundant during the 1945–1965 striper boom. This was the era of the big striper, and these lures took an incredible number of large fish.

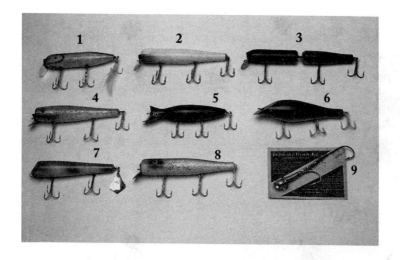

Pictured from left to right:

1. *Connecticut Yankee Lure, made by Walter "Kris" Krystock of Meriden, Connecticut. This was designed for a long cast.*

2. *Blue Streak Lure. This surf lure in yellow was an old favorite of beach fishermen. Made in Waltham, Massachusetts. The company made two sizes of poppers and swimmers.*

3. *Mureel (jointed lure) Made by Charlie Murat Tackle Shop in North Smithfield, Rhode Island. This is the giant jointed eel that Charlie was famous for.*

4. *Captain Bill Lure. First made in Rhode Island and shortly after, the company changed hands and was Massachusetts based and distributed by the Red Top Tackle Shop of Buzzards Bay, Massachusetts.*

5. *Stan Gibbs GS3 Lure. A famous bottle plug designed by the famous fisherman from Sagamore, Massachusetts. Stan Gibbs was well known as an outstanding fisherman in his day and an innovator of numerous successful saltwater lures, including the swimmer made for night fishing. The earlier lures had brass wire through the lure as does this one. This lure dates back to the early sixties or seventies.*

6. *Floyd Roman lure. Made by Floyd Roman of Three Rivers, Massachusetts. The Lures Roman made varied from tiny eel lures weighing less than an ounce all the way up to the largest surf sizes shown here.*

7. *Fishmaster Flaptail lure. Originally made by Rhode Island fishing legend Jerry Sylvester and later by the Fishmaster Sporting Goods Company of Wollaston, Massachusetts. This surface flaptail lure was a must-have lure during the World War II striper fishing era.*

8. *Goo-Goo-Eye lure. Just one of many varieties of striper lures made in Stamford, Connecticut. This model is the earliest, with raised tack eyes.*

9. *Chandler's Eelskin Rig. For casting and trolling from a boat. This rig was made with an antibacklash feature to prevent fouling of the skin when casting.*

11

The Proof of the Pudding: Beginners' Skill

I T WAS AN EXCITING SURF-FISHING GUIDED TRIP FOR ME AND two novice surfcasters, one from this side of the globe and the other from the United Kingdom. This is a picture of Englishman Brian Sheardown from North Kelsey, Lincolnshire, England, with his first keeper striped bass of thirty-five pounds caught on a live eel at night.

This was Brian's first guided fishing trip to the USA. He reached me by contacting *Field & Stream* magazine. The editors there contacted *SaltWater Sportsman* magazine where then Associate Editor Curt Garfield got Brian and me together for a trip here in the US.

Brian insisted he would wear a sport jacket and tie with dignity and pride when surf fishing with me, which is a tradition in the UK, where he is a retired honey farmer. He was astonished and happy to catch this fall striper from Chatham Beach on Cape Cod.

Most ardent US surfcasters would be happy to catch this size striper after many years fishing, but it took Brian just three casts to get the job done.

Not all prime striped bass fishing is at night. I guided retired engineer Gene Cabana to his first hefty keeper striped bass on an out-

Brian Sheardown of Lincolnshire, England with a nice striper taken at Chatham Beach on Cape Cod.

going tide in midafternoon. We were wading on a sandbar and casting into a channel near Chatham Light in June, 2000.

Cabana, a resident of Plymouth, Massachusetts and retired after 28 years at GTE, enjoys sport fishing the Cape Cod Canal, Cape Cod Bay, and Chatham Lighthouse, near the Coast Guard Station. He remembers his first trip with me fondly.

"My first trip with Ron was to Chatham Light, an exciting adventure with a stellar view of the Atlantic Ocean," Cabana recalled. "On this beautiful, clear day, the birds were in abundance and diving for sand eels, our first clue that stripers were nearby and success was a possibility.

Gene Cabana of Plymouth, Massachusetts with his first trophy bass at Chatham Light, Cape Cod.

"It was a sunny, clear, warm, day, high noon, and an outgoing tide, that gave me a perfect opportunity to cast my Ron Arra XRA 1322 custom-wrapped surf rod made by a local tackle shop. It was mounted with an Ambassadeur Abu Garcia 7000 C3 reel.

"On my second cast, a hungry striped bass devoured my sand eel. The rod bent very quickly and line started peeling out of my reel as I pulled the rod out of the sand spike and set the hook. Within fifteen minutes, a tired fish, my first keeper bass ever, was successfully beached.

"We caught six other keepers, but this was the largest and it climaxed a perfect day. Many people walked up with their families to marvel at this large fish that was bigger than they were. This was probably the first trophy fish they had seen in their young lives.

"For me it was a thrilling experience that I'll remember for a lifetime. The fun to have Ron Arra along as a wonderful friend and five-star fisherman and my first keeper made this day so special in my life."

Editor's Note: Besides being a professional surfcasting guide and casting instructor on Cape Cod, Ron Arra is a saltwater product design consultant for the Lamiglas Corporation which markets the Ron Arra Signature Series. In 1997 he designed the Ron Arra Surf Pro spinning model which won best in class at the 1997 American Fishing Tackle Manufacturers Association (AFTMA) show.

12

The
Tournament
Trail

S OONER OR LATER, IN ANY SPORT, THE SPECTER OF COMPETI-
tion raises its shaggy head. Nobody with any kind of athletic
background (and yes, fishermen are athletes) can resist the tempta-
tion to find out just how good he or she really is. Distance Casting
tournaments are the place to find out.

In the United States most tournaments allow each caster three at-
tempts and count the longest of the three that lands in-bounds. All
competitors are required to use a 50-pound shock leader. Standard
sinker weight in the US is 5¼ ounces.

Sportcast USA sponsors a series of tournaments in spring and
early summer up and down the Atlantic seaboard, climaxed with the
National Championships, generally at Lewes, Delaware, every May.
There are many local competitions as well. It's a good idea to take in
a couple of events as a spectator before you decide to make the investment in equipment and practice time that it takes to become a
serious tournament caster.

And we're talking a serious investment. Tournament rod blanks
start at around $300 and go upwards from there. You'll need two or

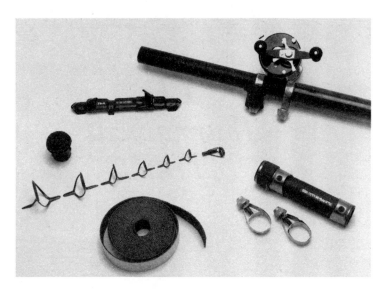

Some components of a tournament casting rod, clockwise from upper left: Fuji FS-7SB reel seat; Abu 6000C reel mounted on rod butt with English reel clamps (note the reducer fitted into the rod butt behind the reel); Fuji FPSD reel seat; English reel clamps; 1/32-inch cork tape; Fuji BNLG guides for conventional rods; rubber butt cap. (Patrick Wiseman photo.)

three tournament reels, which we'll discuss in depth later, and there are hidden expenditures such as the cost of replacing line. Consider that every time you backlash (and even the best of us do that a lot) three hundred yards of line generally has to go back on the reel. You'll go through a bulk spool of line in a hurry if you put in as much practice time as you should.

As we've already mentioned in the introduction, tournament Distance Casting equipment is designed specifically for competition. Most serious tournament casters use competition blanks made in England by Zziplex. They range from thirteen and a half to fourteen feet in length with a very limber tip and an extremely stiff butt section.

You can order them ready made, but most casters prefer to attach their own guides and rod clamp, spacing them to suit their particular style. Casters with small hands will need a reducer, a twelve inch length of smaller-diameter fiberglass that fits onto the rod butt and holds the reel while allowing the caster to get a firm grip and apply pressure on the reel spool with the left hand and thumb.

You won't find very many larger-diameter, revolving-spool saltwater reels on a tournament casting field. Most serious competitors start with smaller bait-casting reels equipped with some sort of magnetic antibacklash device as mentioned earlier, and then make some simple standard modifications. My tournament reels are 6500C3CTMAG centrifugal brake block Abu Garcia Magnetics which have had the level-wind mechanism replaced with a solid crossbar, and four of the eight magnets in the antibacklash mechanism removed. I make adjustment easier by gluing a small cork to the backlash control button on the left side of the reel. Other tournament casters use caps from toothpaste tubes, which work just as efficiently.

Today's top tournament reels include the Blue Yonder, the Ultra-Mag XL3 and the 6500C3CT MAG, all from Abu Garcia.

The reel is also positioned differently on a tournament rod. Instead of being in the normal position halfway along the grip, it is clamped in place six inches from the end of the reducer with English-style screw clamps. There should be just enough room below the reel for the left hand to grip the reducer. Note in this case that the spool is released with the left thumb rather than the right.

Before we get into the cast itself, let's talk about safety for a minute. On a seven hundred-foot cast the sinker is leaving the rod tip at speeds close to two hundred miles an hour. It's going faster than that on a break-off, which means that for all intents and purposes, it's a $5\frac{1}{4}$-ounce bullet. Keep that in mind when you pick a place to practice.

Setting Up—Before I start the cast, I make it a point to double-check my reel setup. My left thumb is covered by a neoprene rubber thumb guard (I cut it from an old Arctic glove) that has ridges so that the reel will not slip under the tremendous amount of pressure I'm creating during the cast until I'm ready to release the line. The line should leave from the left side of the reel, opposite from where my thumb will rest, with three turns of the shock leader around the arbor of the reel spool and the shocker knot (connecting the shock leader and running line) tucked in at the left side of the spool. The reel should be filled to within a sixteenth of an inch of the top. (Patrick Wiseman photo.)

THE TOURNAMENT CAST

The starting position. My left hand is wrapped around the reducer with my thumb on the reel spool and my index finger around the reel clamp's coaster. The rod butt is tucked under my right armpit, and my right hand is extended up the rod with my elbow slightly bent. This method gives a balanced grip for leverage, holding the rod at a forty-five degree angle.

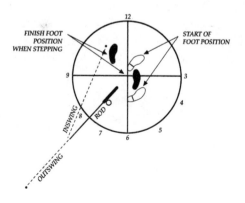

The start of the outswing. I'm holding the rod almost vertically and tipping it out slightly with my right hand to start the sinker in a pendulum motion. Note that the outswing is more exaggerated here than in the other pendulum casts we've described, but the sinker still goes no higher than the tip of the rod on the outswing.

Now I've extended my right arm from the previous vertical position to move the tip of the rod away from the body towards the direction of the outswing. This is done by pulling the rod upward with the left hand to start the motion of the sinker.

The sinker is at the apex of the outswing, but not above the tip of the rod. I'm also starting to pull back on the rod gently before the sinker drops from its apex.

I am moving the rod to my right and pulling upward with my right hand and pushing down with my left. Weight is transferred to the right leg for good balance.

(111)

The sinker is at its apex, which is the highest point of the inswing. At this time there is a slight pause before pulling the rod through the pendulum cast. You will feel a slight tug from the sinker reaching its apex, when the inswing is done correctly. This is the time to start pulling the rod through with the body very slowly before the rod unlocks its prebending action. The left leg is also being pulled to the left to let the body come around in a smooth motion.

Rod continues to move and compress, with the left leg moving to the left, which will bring the body around to the cast for a slow build up of power and compression of the rod.

Rod position has dropped parallel to the field. Weight is now transferred to both legs for balance and control. The left leg is placed completely to the left, so the body will follow through, twisting at the waist. The head has turned in the direction of the cast, with the body and the head upward for good balance. Rod is beginning to compress and load even more now.

Rod is into the power stroke, being pulled around by the left hand, and the whole body is moving in sequence.

(113)

Rod is in correct lever position, with power mostly coming from body and legs. This is the time you want to have the feeling of being underneath the rod, pulling down with the left hand and punching upwards with the right hand.

Rod is in a fully loaded, compressed, and locked position by coming up into the rod punching up with the right hand and pulling down with the left creating a powerful lever action for increased casting distance.

Body position is now upward, positioned for the final stages of the full tournament pendulum cast. Rod is unloading and bringing the sinker overhead with tremendous speed and power for release. Body weight is completely transferred to the left leg at this time.

Follow through with the cast with the rod tip in the direction of the sinker in line to reduce any friction that may be encountered at the final stages of touchdown.

Controlling the cast—If there's one thing that you never want to do under any circumstances in a tournament cast it's to thumb the spool once the sinker is on its way. That's a quick ticket to the biggest backlash you'll ever see and a certain break-off.

I start turning the cork attached to the Ultra MAG XL3 backlash control button clockwise, moving the magnets away from the spool to reduce the eddy current created by the magnets when the sinker has been on its way for approximately two seconds. This keeps the reel from overrunning as the sinker starts to reach peak speed.

This is an art that takes a lot of practice, and you'll get your share of backlashes, but keep at it until it's second nature. Sometimes it's that little bit of fine tuning that will translate into those two or three extra feet that will win a tournament.

13

Tune Up for
More Distance

OWNING A FIRST-CLASS DISTANCE-CASTING OUTFIT IS LIKE driving a high-performance race car. In order to get the most out of it, you have to tune it correctly on a regular basis.

In the hands of top tournament casters, spool speed in a well-tuned reel can exceed 30,000 revolutions per minute. These reels are all capable of sending a 5¼ ounce lead weight over eight hundred feet, going after striped bass in deep water past the breakers, or competing for high honors on the tournament field. These reels are engineered to handle the tremendous torque of casting great distances.

Tuning techniques for two of the most popular distance reels follow:

From left to right:
1. Abu Garcia Ambassadeur 6500C3 CT Blue Yonder, 5.3:1 gear ratio, 190 yards of 17-pound test; 2. Abu Garcia Ambassadeur 6500C3 CT MAG 5.3:1 gear ratio; 190 yards 17-pound test; 3. Abu Garcia Ambassadeur 6000 C, 5.1 gear ratio 300 Yards 12-pound test; 4. Abu Garcia Ambassadeur Ultra MAG XL 3 modified version, 300 yards 12-pound test.

TUNING THE ABU 6500 C3 CT MAG

The Abu 6500C3 CT MAG is one of the most popular tournament casting reels today and a top performer for distance casting around the world. Here are four basic methods of tuning and control to get the utmost performance of the reel for tournament casting.

First of all, choice of oil is very important in being able to control the Abu in a tournament. If you use oil that is too thin, the reel will require more centrifugal brake blocks or more magnets and less line level. If you use fewer magnets then you will need thicker oil and more brake blocks.

Tuning can get complicated for the novice distance surfcaster, so I hope this introduction will give a better understanding about tuning the Abu 6500C series reels, whether equipped with magnets or centrifugal brake blocks.

The same rules apply to the Abu 6500C3 CT Blue Yonder Model reel, a top choice among tournament casters in the UK and here in America. It has no magnets, only brake blocks.

CENTRIFUGAL BRAKE BLOCKS

You can adjust the magnets during the cast, but you cannot adjust the brake blocks. A good way to start is to use two small brake blocks until you get a better feel of how the reel's tuning matches your ability and style of casting.

You will have to balance your centrifugal brake blocks with the magnets for top performance, depending on your style and power. Later on, when your casting style smooths out, you can go with one brake block, or try none.

MAGNETS

Use four magnets to start out with, just to get the feel. When you start developing a smoother cast, then I suggest using three magnets with less magnet braking power. The magnets are held in place with a metal plate by magnetism only. There are seven spaces for the magnets to fit in place, but the factory has four or five fitted already.

Make sure you reposition the magnets in the center of the plate rather than at each end. This will create a good balance of magnetism. I have found that with my smooth style of casting the slide adjustment works best for me when set between positions three and four at the start of the cast. Under ideal conditions with no wind, move the slide adjustment slowly to zero, once the lead is on its way (about halfway through the cast) to touchdown.

OILING BEARINGS

Apply two drops of Yellow Label Rocket Fuel in each hot bearing. Use the same oil that came with the reel box, in the clear plastic tube with a red stripe marked on it. Carefully remove the bearings from the spool and use the same method that I used for the Abu 7000 C3 level-wind model reel elsewhere in this book. If you find that you need lighter oil because the reel is running too slowly for your style of casting, try replacing the oil with the Tournament Grade Rocket Fuel that is popular among tournament casters.

Line Level

Line leveling procedure utilizes 12-pound-test Golden Stren line, which has a diameter of 0.35mm. If you're using a premium tournament casting line that is copolymer, fill to the top of the spool and add twenty to thirty more feet of line after a few practice casts and stretching the line with the sinker imbedded in the ground. Make sure your magnetic adjustment is set between eight and six for the first few practice casts, then switch back to four for the ultimate long cast.

When using the new thinner-diameter line, such as the current regulation USA standard tournament line (0.32mm diameter), keep the line level to the top of the spool or just slightly below, depending on wind, humidity, and temperature conditions.

Spool Balance

It is imperative that the reel spool be balanced for a long cast on the tournament field. The spool from the manufacturer is true and balanced coming out of the reel box, leaving one less thing to worry about. That said, the first few turns of line on the spool determine whether a spool performs and runs smoothly with hardly a sound or rattles and clunks like a coffee grinder.

Make sure the first wrap of line is to one side of the spool with its knot tucked up to the right. Continue to wind the line on the spool in cotton reel fashion, meaning each turn is against the one before with no overlap. Keep doing this until across the spool, then continue to retrieve line evenly and level until filled at the correct level, and snip.

After snipping the line place Scotch tape or plastic tape twice around the line end where you first started your knot and turn. It must be an even overlap because the tape will cause the spool to become unbalanced. Next, slide the magnetic adjustment to zero, which is all the way off. After this procedure, tighten the star drag system and give the handle a good fast flip, being careful not to drop the reel. Now put it in free spool with the spool rotating as fast as you can. If the line was laid level, there should be no sound or vibration.

If you have some vibration, try rewinding your line and knot on the opposite side of the spool and repeat the procedure. After about one hundred not-so-powerful, smooth practice casts, most often any vibration from the spool will be eliminated. I will repeat that the first twenty yards of line laid on the spool is very important for a smooth-running reel that can be the difference between victory and defeat in a casting tournament. Good luck.

Left to right:

Hair dryer; reel grease; tournament casting Reel Rocket Oil; 3-in-One SAE 20-wt blue can; Abu 6500C3-CT Blue Yonder reel, dismantled; 7000C3 left side plate; right side plate; spool; centrifugal brake blocks; adjustable caps; ball bearings on wire; clean dust-free cotton cloth.

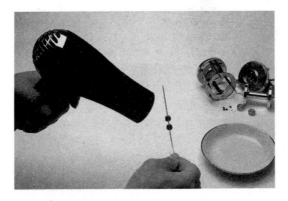

Heating Bearings

Cleaning– Spraying WD 40 into shield of bearings.

Oiling bearings.

Replacing centrifugal brake blocks.

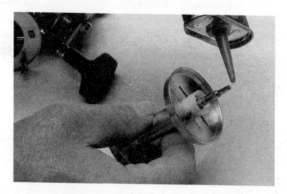

Placing oil onto spindles.

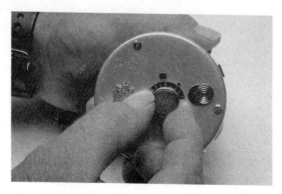

Adjusting right side adjustment cap to V-shaped indicator for side play of spool.

CLEANING, OILING, AND TUNING THE ABU 7000 C3

The Abu 7000-C3 is a great all-around Heavy Duty surfcasting reel. Here's how to clean, oil, and tune it.

First of all, remove all line from the spool. Then remove the three screws from the right side plate of the reel. These often can be loosened by hand or with a flathead screwdriver.

Be sure to hold the reel in a vertical position as you remove the right side plate. Here you will see the four centrifugal brake blocks. Remove the spool and shake the brake blocks loose and set them aside. Remove the left side adjustment cap, exposing the ball bearing. Remove the lock wire with a small flat screwdriver.

Tap on the back side of the bearing and it will fall out of place. Now that you have removed the left side bearing, it is time to remove the right side bearing. Loosen and remove the adjustment cap. Tap the back of the right side plate, and the bearing should fall out on its own. Bearings that have old oil in them should be cleaned.

Place the two ball bearings in a dish and spray the ball bearings with WD-40 making sure to spray into the shield of the bearing. Now, place the bearings on a wire, and heat them with a hair dryer at its hottest setting. This will loosen old oil and grease. Touch the ball bearings to make sure they are hot but be careful that you don't overheat them!

Place the ball bearings back into the dish and spray them again with WD-40 into the shield. Place the bearings back on the wire and heat them again, repeating the process. As soon as they are hot to touch, place them on a lint-free tissue. Place two drops of 3-in-One, 20 weight into each bearing. The oil will not soak into the bearing shield if it is not hot.

Now, install the left side bearing into the left side plate and lock the bearing in with the wire clip by snapping it into its groove. Screw the adjustment cap back on and place the second ball bearing into position on the right side plate where the handle is located. There is no wire clip here to lock the bearing in.

Now, replace the adjustment cap by screwing it on. To install the spool make sure to clean both left and right spool spindles with lint-free tissue paper or a clean cotton cloth. Make sure before installing the spool that each tip of the spindle has one drop of oil on it. Keep the reel cage vertical to install the spool back into its side plates.

With the right side of the spool exposed, install only two break blocks back on the spool pins opposite each other. Now, install the right side plate and snug all screws by hand, then tighten easily with a screwdriver, making sure not to tighten too much because of the possibility of distorting the side plate.

Now, place the reel into free spool, (the left side adjustment cap will be loose) and start to turn the adjustment cap clockwise to tighten against the spool spindle until you see the spool rotate in the same direction then stop. Now counterclockwise, turn the adjustment cap the opposite way until the spool stops rotating. Then you are done adjusting.

This adjustment will stop the horizontal movement of the spool. For greater casting distances turn the adjustment counterclockwise, so there is scant side play for increased distance at the final stage of the cast.

The final adjustment will mark your setting by aligning the small tab indicator on the left side plate to the V-shaped indicator on the adjustment cap. This will establish a benchmark setting for future infield adjustment of the tension against the spool spindles.

From this starting point you can add or decrease tension on the spool to prevent backlashes or to help further your cast. Replace line-level on the spool to within an eighth of an inch of the top of the flange.

Appendix A

SOURCES FOR EQUIPMENT

Rods for Distance Casting Tournaments

Zziplex Ltd., Units 1 and 2, Mountfield Road Industrial Estate, New Romney Kent, TN28 8LY, ENGLAND. Phone 011–44–1797–366–602. Fax 011–44–1797–366–751

Sinkers Designed for Distance

D.C.A. Moulds, SA4 The Maltings, East Tyndall Street, Cardiff, CF1 5EA, ENGLAND

Distance Rods for Fishing

Abu Garcia, Inc., Pure Fishing, 1900 18th Street, Spirit Lake Iowa, 51360 Phone 712–336–1520

Daiwa Corp., Daiwa Seiko Inc., 12851 Midway Place, Cerritos, CA 90703. Tel. 562–802–9589.

Lamiglas, P.O. Box 1000, Woodland, WA 98674. Tel. 360–225–9436

Penn Fishing Tackle Manufacturing Company, 3028 West Hunting Park Avenue, Philadelphia, PA 19132. Phone 215–229–9415.

Reels for Distance Casting

Abu Garcia, Inc., Pure Fishing, 1900 18th Street, Spirit Lake, Iowa, 51360 Tel. 712–336–1520

Daiwa Corp., Daiwa Seiko Inc., 12851 Midway Place, Cerritos, CA 90703. Tel. 562–802–9589.

Penn Fishing Tackle Manufacturing Company, 3028 West Hunting Park Avenue, Philadelphia, PA 19132. 215–229–9415

Shimano American Corporation, One Holland, Irvine, CA 92618. Phone 949–951–5003

Van Staal Inc., 366 Sniffens Lane, Stratford, CT 06615. Phone 203–380–0607

CONTACT THE AUTHOR

ronarra@lamiglas.com

Appendix B

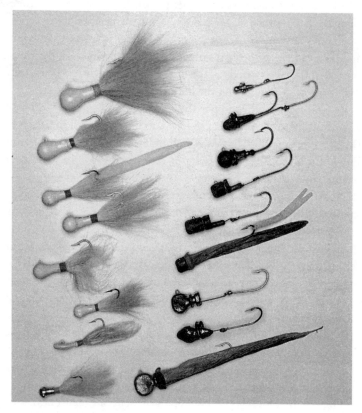

Left from top—bucktail jigs:
8 ounces; 5 ounces; 2½-ounce jig with pork rind; 4 ounces; 3 ounces; 1½ ounces; 1-ounce slider jig for sandy bottom; ¾-ounce light-tackle jig.
Right from top—eelskin rigs:
½ ounce; 2½ ounces; 4 ounces; 3 ounces; 4 ounces; 2-ounce rig with eelskin and pork rind; 3 ounces; 4 ounces; 4-ounce rig with eelskin.

FISHING THE JIG AND EEL

When there is moving water over structure with rips building up and different speeds of current, the jig and eelskin rig become very productive lures night or day. These lures are not newcomers, in fact they have been catching striped bass and other gamefish for almost six decades along the banks of the Cape Cod Canal and many other places.

The jig and eelskin rig are very productive when cast upcurrent and bounced along the bottom with a lifelike action. Jerk the tip of the rod at different speeds as the lure travels downcurrent, hopefully without getting hung up on the bottom.

Avoiding getting hung up is the tricky part of jigging. It will help a great deal and catch more fish if you use a nonstretch line such as Berkley FireLine, Berkley Whiplash braided line, or Berkley Power Pro. Using these lines for jigging or eel skinning will increase your control and feel for the bottom.

Nonstretch lines have much better bite detection and more abrasion resistance and strength for their diameter, as well as better hook setting capability.

The speed of the current will determine the weight of the jig or eelskin used. As the tide starts to change, the slower current calls for a lighter jig, maybe one-and-a-half to two ounces, while a fast-moving current may require three to four ounces to reach the bottom and bounce correctly.

It takes some practice and dedication to acquire the feel for the correct action to the jig or eelskin so it attracts fish. At first there will be some lures lost below, but chalk those up to experience. I have seen even ardent jig fishermen lose a few to the bottom.

The rod used for jigging should be a conventional, but I have seen some good jig fishermen who insist on using spinning models. A rod from nine and a half feet to ten and a half feet rated for three to four ounces or four to six ounces of lead and with medium-heavy or heavy action and a firm butt section works best for casting distance, feeling the bouncing jig, and setting the hook.

The reel that I use on my jigging and eelskinning rod is the Abu 7000C3 filled with fifty-pound-test FireLine and three feet of forty-pound-test mono as a leader attached to the FireLine with a heavy-duty barrel swivel using the double clinch knot. A single strong snap is attached to the jig. My favorite jigging rod is a custom-built-conventional Lamiglas XRA 126 1MH, ten and a half feet, rated for four- to six-ounce lures.

To rig an eelskin, place it over hooks by pulling the skin toward the head of the rig. Then pull the point of hook through eelskin rig. Next step is to tie skin at leadhead groove with thread or dental floss. Wrap several turns around and then tie off using a square knot. Make sure there is a half-inch overlap of eelskin at the head of jig.

Appendix C

FOR THE RECORD

National Championships Won By Ron Arra, and national record casts.

1983 DuPont Stren National Open; First American man to cast beyond 600' using 0.35mm line with a 4oz weight: 636'-6" Lewes, Del.

1984 DuPont Stren National Championship; cast of 676", 1" 5¼ oz weight, Lewes Del.

1985 DuPont Stren National Championship; cast of 656' 5¼ oz weight. Phoenix, Ariz.

1986 DuPont Stren National Championship; cast of 656', 5¼ oz weight. Harrisburg, Pa.

1988 DuPont Stren National Championships, cast of 738'.15, 5¼ oz weight.(New Record Cast) Marco Island, Fla.

OTHER NATIONAL RECORD CASTS

1987 August 30, SportCast USA , New England Casting Championships; cast of, 758',4". Falmouth, Ma Cape Cod.

DuPont Stren New England Regional Casting Championships, April 6,1985 cast of 737'-11". Falmouth Ma. Cape Cod. First American to cast beyond 700' using 0.35mm diameter line.

1988 DuPont Stren New England Regional Casting Championships, cast of 738'.08, 5 1/4 oz weight, Falmouth Ma. Cape Cod.

Index

A

Abu Garcia
  address and phone number, 127
  tournament reels, 107
Abu Garcia 7000
  picture of, 7
Abu Garcia Blue Yonder
  tournament reels, 107
Abu Garcia 5500C
  revolving spool, 6
Abu Garcia 6000C
  picture, 106
Abu Garcia 6000C3
  cleaning, oiling and tuning,
    124–125
Abu Garcia 7000C, 6
Abu Garcia 7000C3
  picture of, 7
Abu Garcia 7500C3
  picture of, 7
Abu Garcia 6500C3CT, 6
Abu Garcia 7500C3CT, 6
Abu Garcia 6500C3CT MAG
  tournament reels, 107
  tuning, 118–123
Abu Garcia Ultra-Mag XL3
  tournament reels, 107
Accuracy
  casting, 57
Action blank, 4
Adjustment cap
  adjusting, 123
Aerodynamic lures
  for casting, 56
Albright special, 67

Alconite guides
  attaching reels to rods, 6
Arra, Ray Sr., 79
Arra, Ron
  my first catch, 77–80
  National Championships won, 133
  record casts, 133
  saltwater product design
    consultant, 104
Atom Ketch'n Fetch
  picture and description, 63, 64
Atom Popper
  picture and description, 63, 64
  picture of, 10

B

Backcast, 91–95
Bait rigs, 62
Barrel swivel, 61, 62
Beach fishing trip
  basic equipment, 8
Bearings
  cleaning, 122
  heating, 122
  oiling, 122
Beginners
  start off right, 77–82
Beginners' skill, 101–104
Berkley Trilene 30-pound-test
  picture of, 12
Berkley Whiplash 50-pound-test
  picture of, 12
Bill Upperman's jig
  picture and description, 65
  picture of, 10

Blanks
  tournament rod
    cost, 105
    types, 4
Blue Streak Lure
  picture and description, 99
Blue Yonder. *See also* Abu Garcia
  tournament reels, 107
Body motion
  for casting, 56–57
BogaGrip, 75
Bomber swimmer
  picture and description, 64
Bomber swimming lure
  picture of, 10
Bucktail jigs
  picture, 129

C
Cabana, Gene, 101–104
Canal cast
  technique, 24–28
Captain Bill Lure
  picture and description, 99
Carroll, Terry, 13
Casting. *See also* Distance casting
  accuracy, 57
  aerodynamic lures, 56
  body motion, 56–57
  canal
    technique, 24–28
  centrifugal brake-block, 54
  field-type pendulum, 17
  light tackle
    technique, 39–42
  lines, 54–55
  long-distance, 61, 71–75
  lures, 56
  magnetically controlled reel, 54
  modified pendulum, 17
    reels for, 6
    technique, 33–38
  night fishing, 58

off-the-beach
  technique, 19–23
overhead beach
  technique, 29–32
practice, 58
reel position, 52
reels, 54
rods, 52–54
roll, 86–90
  rods, 84
spinning guides, 52
spool, 54
techniques, 19–46
  foot position, 20
  starting position, 15
tournament, 109–116
  gear suggested for, 6
  knot, 70
  rod components, 106
  rod design, 3
wading pendulum
  technique, 41–46
weather, 57–58
wind, 57
Centrifugal brake-block
  for casting, 54
  replacing, 123
  tuning, 119
Chandler's Eelskin Rig
  picture and description,
    99–100
Children
  start off right, 77–82
Chunk bait rig, 62
Clamps
  English reel
    picture, 106
Connecticut Yankee Lure
  picture and description, 99
Conventional surfcasting reels, 7
Crackoffs, 18
Creek Chub popper
  picture and description, 64

D
Daiwa
  address and phone number, 127
Daiwa Emblem 5500 A, 6
  picture of, 9
Daiwa Emblem-X 6000 T, 6
  picture of, 9
D.C.A. moulds
  address and phone number, 127
Distance casting. *See also* Casting;
    Long-distance casting
  equipment, 106
  parts of, 51
  reels, 127–128
    tuning technique, 117–125
  rods
    fishing, 127
  sinkers, 127
  tips for more, 51–59
  tune up for more, 117–125
Distance Casting tournament,
    105–116
  rods for, 127
Drop length
  canal cast, 24
  characteristics, 16
  foot position, 20
  rod position, 20

E
Eddystone Eel dropper
  picture and description, 64
Eelskinning
  gear to use, 11
Eelskinning rod
  reel, 130
Eelskin rigs
  fishing with, 130–131
  picture, 129
English reel clamps
  picture, 106
English-style Baitsafe lure
  picture and description, 63

English-style two-handers, 83
Equipment
  sources, 127–128
Extra fast action blank, 4

F
Fast action blank, 4
Field-type pendulum cast, 17
Filling
  revolving-spool reel, 66
  spinning reel, 66
Fishing
  jig and eel, 130–131
Fishing reel
  picture of, 9
Fishing situation
  gear suggested for, 6
Fishing technique
  twang, 72
Fishmaster Flaptail lure
  picture and description,
    99–100
Flies
  for two-handed fly rods, 95
Float rig, 62
Floyd Roman lure
  picture and description, 99
Fly rods, 83–95
Footing
  canal cast, 25
Foot position
  backcast, 91
  canal cast, 24
  light-tackle surfcasting, 39
  modified, 33
  overhead beach cast, 29
  roll casting, 87
  for tournament casting, 109
  WPC, 41
Fuji Alconite VMNAG ring guides,
    13
Fuji BNLG
  attaching reels to rods, 6

Fuji Concept Alconite guides
  attaching reels to rods, 6
Fuji FPSD Deluxe low-profile reel
  seat
  attaching reels to rods, 6
Fuji FPSD reel seat
  picture, 106
Fuji FS-7SB
  attaching reels to rods, 6
Fuji FS-7SB reel seat
  picture, 106
Fuji NSG
  attaching reels to rods, 6
Fuji PST silicon carbide
  attaching reels to rods, 6

G
Gag's grabber Bluefish Bomb
  picture and description, 63
GBSVLG
  attaching reels to rods, 6
Gear, 3–13
  tacking care of, 47–50
Gibbs, Stan, 17, 97–100
Gibbs Needlefish
  picture of, 10
Gibbs Pencil Popper
  picture of, 10
Gibbs Redhead Polaris Popper
  picture of, 10
Goo-Goo-Eye lure
  picture and description, 99–100
Gripper tool, 75
Guides
  Alconite
    attaching reels to rods, 6
  recommended, 13
Guide spacing
  recommended, 13

H
Habs popper
  picture of, 10

Habs Squid Popper
  picture of, 10
Hand gaff, 75
Hand size
  and rods, 107
High-sticking, 73
Holden, John, 2
  principle of pendulum cast, 15
Hooks
  cleaning, 49
  sharpening, 50

I
Improved clinch knot, 69
Inswing
  description, 17
  modified, 33
  MPC, 35, 36
  for tournament casting, 109,
    112
  WPC, 44, 45

J
Jigging
  gear to use, 11
  rod used for, 130
Jigging bucktails, 61
Jigs
  cleaning, 49
Joining lines, 68
Jointed lure
  picture and description, 99

K
Kids
  start off right, 77–82
Knives
  sharpening, 50

L
Lamiglas
  address and phone number, 127
  rods designed

modified pendulum technique,
3
Lamiglas blanks
actions, 4
Lamiglas conventional WRA 1322,
5
Lamiglas spinning model SXRA
1083
light-tackle surfcasting, 39
Lamiglas three-piece
two-handed fly rod, 85
Lamiglas XRA 1083, 5
Lamiglas XRA 1205, 5
Lamiglas XRA 1322, 5
Lamiglas XRA conventional 126
LMH, 5
Lamiglas X RA 132 2 li Rod
off-the-beach cast, 19
Leaders, 63
characteristics, 16, 17
extra tips, 59
shock, 17, 63
tying, 67
Leadhead bucktail jig
picture and description, 65
Leadhead surf jig
picture of, 10
Lemon juice
sharpening, 50
Light tackle cast
technique, 39–42
Light tackle lures
picture of, 10
Line level
tuning, 120
Lines
for casting, 54–55
joining, 68
Live eel rig, 62
Locked, 17
Long-distance casting
long-distance fishing, 61
vs. long-distance fishing, 71

playing technique, 71–75
Long-distance fishing
long-distance casting, 61
vs. long-distance casting, 71
Long two-handed Spey rods, 83
Lures
for casting, 56
cleaning, 49

M
Magnetically controlled reel
for casting, 54
Magnets
tuning, 119
Moderate action blank, 4
Modified pendulum cast, 17
reels for, 6
technique, 33–38
Monofilament line, 49
Mureel
picture and description, 99

N
Newell P220, 6
picture of, 7
Night fishing
casting, 58
Novice
equipment suggestions, 81
start off right, 77–82

O
Off-the-beach cast
technique, 19–23
Oiling bearings
tuning, 119–120
One-handed fly rod
vs. two-handed fly rod, 84
Outswing
canal cast, 25
description, 17
modified, 33
MPC, 35

Outswing *(continued)*
  technique, 34
  for tournament casting, 109–111
  WPC, 42, 43
Overhead beach cast
  technique, 29–32

P
Palomar knot, 69
Penn
  address and phone number, 127
Penn 140, 6
Penn 650
  picture of, 9
Penn 930 Levelmatic
  gear suggested for, 6
Penn 525 MAG, 6
  picture of, 7
Penn 55OSS
  gear suggested for, 6
Penn 450SS
  gear suggested for, 6
  picture of, 9
Penn 850SS
  gear suggested for, 6
  picture of, 9
Plugs
  gear suggested, 12
Practice
  casting, 58
  choosing place, 18
  right kind, 17

R
Rebel swimmer
  picture of, 10
Reels. *See also* Abu Garcia
  attachment to rod, 6
  for casting, 54
  clamps
    English, 106
  cleaning and oiling, 49
  conventional surfcasting, 7
  cover, 49

distance
  tuning technique, 117–125
distance casting, 127–128
  extra tips, 59
  filling, 55, 66
  fishing
    picture of, 9
  jigging and eelskinning rod, 130
  magnetically controlled
    for casting, 54
  for modified pendulum
    technique, 6
  position
    for casting, 52
  seat (*See* Fuji FPSD reel seat)
  surfcasting
    picture of, 9
  tournament, 107
    Ultra-Mag XL3, 107
  tournament distance-casting
    picture of, 9
Reverse Atom lure
  picture and description, 64
Revolving spool
  Abu Garcia 5500C, 6
Revolving-spool reel
  filling, 66
Rigging
  for that faraway fish, 61–70
Ring size
  recommended, 13
RIO Products
  two-handed fly rod, 85
Roberts lure
  picture and description, 64
Rods
  for casting, 52–54
  distance casting tournament, 127
  length
    for fishing, 72
  position
    backcast, 91
    light-tackle surfcasting, 39
    MPC, 34

overhead beach cast, 29
roll casting, 87
for tournament casting, 109
WPC, 41
Roll casting, 86–90
rods, 84
Ron Arra Spinning Surf Pro Model
XSRA 1321-2, 5
Ron Arra Spinning Surf Pro Model
XSRA 1322-2, 5
Ron Arra Surf Pro Series
Lamiglas, 4

S
Safety, 18
practice area, 107
Salmon rods, 84
Sand eels, 62
Seat
reel (*See* Fuji FPSD reel seat)
Sea worm, 62
Self
tacking care of, 47–50
Setting up
overhead beach cast, 29
Sharpening
lemon juice, 50
Sheardown, Brian, 101–102
Shimano American
address and phone number, 128
Shocker knot, 108
Shock leader, 17, 63
Shorty Hopkins lure
picture and description, 65
Single-hook eelskin rig
picture and description, 65
Sinkers
distance, 127
Slow action blank, 4
Sources
equipment, 127–128
Spey cast, 86–90
Spindles

oiling, 123
Spinning gear
gear suggested for, 6
Spinning guides
for casting, 52
Spinning reel
filling, 66
Spool
for casting, 54
Spool balance
tuning, 120–121
Stan Gibbs GS3 Lure
picture and description, 99
Stan Gibbs Pencil Popper
picture and description, 64
Stan Gibbs Polaris Popper
picture and description, 64
Stan Gibbs Skipper
picture and description, 64
Stan Gibbs Swimmer
picture and description, 64
Super Strike Bullet
picture and description, 63
Super Strike Little Neck Popper
picture and description, 64
Super Strike Needle Fish
picture and description, 65
Surfcasting
gear, 3–13
lines
picture of, 12
reel
picture of, 9
Surf fishing
gear, 3–4
rods, 5
Swinging Swiper
picture and description, 64

T
Tournament casting, 109–116
controlling, 116
gear suggested for, 6

INDEX

Tournament casting *(continued)*
  knot, 70
  outswing, 109–111
  rod components, 106
  setting up, 108
Tournament distance-casting reel
  picture of, 9
Tournament reels, 107
  Ultra-Mag XL3, 107
Tournament rod
  designed for casting only, 3
Tournament rod blanks
  cost, 105
Tournament trail, 105–116
Tuning
  Abu Garcia 6500C3CT MAG,
    118–123
Tuning kit, 121
Tuning technique
  distance reels, 117–125
Twang, 72
Two-handed fly rod, 83–95
  hand position, 85
  line, 85
  vs. one-handed model, 84

U
Ultra-Mag XL3. *See also* Abu
    Garcia
  tournament reels, 107
Uni-Knot circle, 68

V
Van Staal
  address and phone number, 128
Van Staal VS100
  gear suggested for, 6

Van Staal VS200
  picture of, 9
Van Staal VS250
  gear suggested for, 6

W
Wading pendulum cast
  technique, 41–46
Warming up, 47
Weather
  casting, 57–58
Wind
  for casting, 57
WindCutter
  two-handed fly rod, 85
Wrist weights, 48

X
XRA 1083, 5
XRA 1205, 5
XRA 1322, 5
XRA conventional 126 LMH, 5

Y
Youngsters
  start off right, 77–82
Yourself
  tacking care of, 47–50

Z
Zziplex, 13, 106
  address and phone number, 127
Zzpilex Primo Phase Taper
  tournament rod, 13